P9-ELS-683

Slow Gardening

**A No-Stress
Philosophy
for All Senses
and Seasons**

FELDER RUSHING

Foreword by Roger B. Swain

CHELSEA GREEN PUBLISHING

WHITE RIVER JUNCTION, VERMONT

green press
INITIATIVE

Chelsea Green Publishing is committed to preserving ancient forests and natural resources. We elected to print this title on FSC®-certified paper containing at least 10% postconsumer recycled paper, processed chlorine-free. As a result, for this printing, we have saved:

14 Trees (40' tall and 6-8" diameter)
6,177 Gallons of Wastewater
6 million BTUs Total Energy
391 Pounds of Solid Waste
1,370 Pounds of Greenhouse Gases

Chelsea Green Publishing made this paper choice because we are a member of the Green Press Initiative, a nonprofit program dedicated to supporting authors, publishers, and suppliers in their efforts to reduce their use of fiber obtained from endangered forests. For more information, visit www.greenpressinitiative.org.

Environmental impact estimates were made using the Environmental Defense Paper Calculator. For more information visit: www.papercalculator.org.

Project Manager: Patricia Stone
Editorial Contact: Susan Warner
Developmental Editor: Ben Watson
Copy Editor: Cannon Labrie
Proofreader: Nancy Ringer
Indexer: Lee Lawton
Designer: Peter Holm, Sterling Hill Productions

All photographs by Felder Rushing, unless otherwise credited.
Images on pages v, 1, 14, 15, 25, 35, 40, 64, 65, 67, 89, 92, 178, 183, 194, 198, 201, 202, 203, 209, and 210 are from iStockphoto.

Printed in the United States of America
First printing June, 2011
10 9 8 7 6 5 4 3 2 1   11 12 13 14 15

Our Commitment to Green Publishing

Chelsea Green sees publishing as a tool for cultural change and ecological stewardship. We strive to align our book manufacturing practices with our editorial mission and to reduce the impact of our business enterprise in the environment. We print our books and catalogs on chlorine-free recycled paper, using vegetable-based inks whenever possible. This book may cost slightly more because we use recycled paper, and we hope you'll agree that it's worth it. Chelsea Green is a member of the Green Press Initiative (www.greenpressinitiative.org), a nonprofit coalition of publishers, manufacturers, and authors working to protect the world's endangered forests and conserve natural resources. *Slow Gardening* was printed on FSC®-certified paper supplied by QuadGraphics that contains at least 10-percent postconsumer recycled fiber.

Library of Congress Cataloging-in-Publication Data
Rushing, Felder, 1952-
  Slow gardening : a no-stress philosophy for all senses and seasons / Felder Rushing ; foreword by Roger B. Swain.
    p. cm.
  Includes index.
  ISBN 978-1-60358-267-4
1. Gardening--Philosophy. 2. Gardens--Philosophy. I. Title.

SB454.3.P45R87 2011
635.9--dc22

                    2011006357

Chelsea Green Publishing Company
Post Office Box 428
White River Junction, VT 05001
(802) 295-6300
www.chelseagreen.com

FSC
www.fsc.org
MIX
Paper from
responsible sources
FSC® C084269

CONTENTS

FOREWORD:
ROADSIDE ATTRACTIONS

Thanks to Felder Rushing I know the difference between *tacky* and *gaudy*. *Tacky* is having a single pink plastic flamingo stuck in with the geraniums and petunias. *Gaudy* is when you have a flock of twenty-five. What else should I have expected to see as I drove down his street in Jackson, Mississippi? Surely not the neatly mown lawns and the carefully clipped hedges of holly and azalea that front so many of the homes in his part of town.

I have edited Felder, lectured alongside him, shared moonshine, barbecue, and fried peach pies. I have listened to B. B. King on the radio while driving with him past cotton fields and catfish farms on the Mississippi Delta. But I see him all over America. I have seen him in Manassas, Virginia, in a corner lot filled with dahlias and enclosed by a line of riderless bicycles, each painted white and supported by a short section of rebar—a ghost version of the Tour de France. I have seen him in a pack of topiary hounds displayed at the Philadelphia Flower Show, ivy canines circling a fire hydrant. I see him here in New Hampshire, every time I pass the concrete chicken that my love Elisabeth brought home from Indiana in her carry-on.

Felder has been called many things. Slow is not the first that comes to mind. Wildly enthusiastic, yes, inquisitive, and acquisitive. If I had to describe his planting style I would say "think bower bird": if it is bright and shiny—be it a phrase, a plant, or an artifact—he will weave it into the tapestry of his gardens. Sunlight glints from glass bottles, their necks impaled on the branches of his bottle trees. He wrote the book on scarecrows—literally. And he is forever retrieving lost wheels from the roadside from which he fashions tire planters, objets d'art that he considers to be the perfect hostess gifts.

These days Felder drives around the country in a 1988 Ford F-150 pickup painted John Deere green with a garden of rosemary, basil, peppers, juniper, sempervivums, artemisia, and dwarf yuccas rooted right behind the cab—a road-tested assortment that can withstand the buffeting of travel at speeds of seventy-five miles per hour. Along for the ride are his collection of antique English torpedo bottles, a bare-breasted frog figurine, and a wind chime that, at high speed, he admits, sounds "like an ice cream truck on crack."

Felder will be quick to tell you that this book is essentially about pleasing yourself, about following your bliss, about savoring everything that you do in your yard. In theory, the landscape that results might be a garden that is just as formal, just as carefully appointed as the most conservative business suit. Slow Gardening is, by his definition, a very big tent. When you set out to please yourself, however, the result is unlikely to be homogeneity. It's when you worry about keeping up with the neighbors, about preserving property values—that's when you find yourself working with a grimace on your face, and your yard ends up looking all too much like the one next door.

Slow gardens don't have to have bottle trees or iron bathtubs filled with blooming water lilies. There may not be a twelve-foot-tall ferro-cement frog or a ten-ton truck dumping a load of marigolds. Slow gardens don't *have* to be eye-catching, but Felder must know that the best ones are. These are the gardens that cause us to pause, no matter how fast we are passing by. These are the gardens, the ones character-ized by whimsy, that people stop for. The arresting force may be those flamingos, or a herd of plywood Holsteins. The point is that people slow down. They get out of their car. They reach for their camera. They take a picture. And should you, the gardener, be out there at the time, lounging in your hammock, feeding your fish, or just poking at your fire pit, well, then you are about to make a new acquaintance. In the end we are all bound by the alchemy of photosynthesis.

Slow Gardening begins with the individual, yes, and Felder may insist that he gardens for himself. What he is really tending, however, is community. He is saving the world in his own idiosyncratic way—one found cobalt blue bottle at a time.

Roger B. Swain

PREFACE AND ACKNOWLEDGMENTS

Everyone seems to be jumping on the Slow bandwagon started by Italian food activist Carlo Petrini—everywhere we turn there is a new Slow This or Slow That "movement" with guidelines on keeping things simple. But, to me, Slow Gardening is a style, not a bunch of how-to tips. In fact, it is close to being the antithesis of horticulture.

Slow Gardening is more about doing what you enjoy, and *savoring what you do*. Not that this horticulture professor can't make your eyes bleed with horticultural esoterica. But though my take on gardening has been through the hot forge of decades of formal horticulture training and professional work, it's also tempered by my having been raised by real gardeners, including a horticulturist great-grandmother who patiently shared with me her love of wildflowers, a garden-club grandmother whose home-hybridized daylilies won many blue ribbons, another more "country" grandmother who just loved old-fashioned zinnias and her concrete chicken, and my parents, who struggled with vegetables and a lawn while raising a bunch of rowdy kids and pets.

My attitude has also been dragged through countless "behind the scenes" plant safaris into literally every corner of my home country (all fifty states), deep into steamy jungles in both South America and Africa, and from snowy peat bogs of northern Canada to windswept cemeteries on tiny Caribbean islands. I have been on dozens of working garden trips to Europe, and I have lived and gardened on a rural cottage farm in England's western Midlands, a small yard in south Texas, and my own home grounds in the intense heat and humidity of the Mississippi Delta.

I have tended enough gardens of my own to prove that it takes more than knowledge and experience to maintain a nice garden—it often requires planning ahead, investments in plants and tools, and hard work.

In other words, this gardener has had his attitude both inspired and battered. And, through it all, I have tried to deconstruct the science of horticulture and interpret it in the everyday language of "garden variety" gardeners. I have discovered that home gardeners are surprisingly similar all over the world in both their attitudes and their approaches to plain old "dirt" gardening.

All that said, there are simply too many dear friends around the world who have influenced me to even begin to acknowledge them by name—really. Throw in a lot of associations—from the Garden Writers Association of America to the American Horticulture Society (with their focus on youth gardening)—and my work around the country with master gardeners, and there is plenty of inspiration to go around.

However, I can assure you that this book would not be in your hands today without the inspiration of Carlo Petrini, the folks at Chelsea Green Publishing, who work so hard to offer sustainable concepts to people in a troubled world, and the patience and diligent work of my friend and editor, Ben Watson. Thank you all.

Felder's great-grandmother Pearl Townsend Boyer – the über Slow Gardener.

CHAPTER ONE
An Introduction to Slow Gardening

The world is too much with us . . .
Getting and spending, we lay waste our powers:
Little we see in Nature that is ours.
—William Wordsworth

"There are only two kinds of people—those who garden, and those who do not."

When garden writer Henry Mitchell penned those words, he was not writing about *what kinds* of gardeners there are. Truth is, most of us are basically lawn mowers and shrub pruners, with maybe a potted plant or two on the patio to watch through the window while we are glued to the weather announcer on TV.

But all of us need to grow something—*anything*—that depends on us at least a little bit, or as Oklahoma horticulturist Russell Studebaker says, "We'd just as well be sittin' around polishin' our silverware."

And we ought to do it in a way that we enjoy, if not downright savor.

For example, do you know how much time it takes to mow your lawn a single time? Estimate how many times you do it every summer, then multiply it by however many years . . . then ponder this: at the end of your life *you will wish you had some of that time back.*

If you believe that, then it's time to *do something about it now.*

Take control of your life. As Eleanor Roosevelt put it, "Whoever you are, you're the person; wherever you are, that's the place; whatever time it is, that's the time to take action."

Slow Gardening

Gardens are ideas as well as spaces.

Life has lots of pressures—why include them in the garden?

Doing something slowly means savoring what you are doing. Slow Gardening has its inspirational roots in Slow Food, an international movement founded by Italian activist Carlo Petrini and others in the 1980s and dedicated to celebrating and defending traditional, seasonal, and sustainably grown local foods, and the people who produce and prepare them. This movement may have started among food cognoscenti and connoisseurs, but it has unleashed a worldwide wave of support among people from all walks of life, from taro farmers in New Caledonia and Hawaii to Sami reindeer herders above the Arctic Circle.

In recent years the idea of Slow has transcended food (Slow Cities, Slow Medicine, etc.), and it strikes a special chord among gardeners who, though perfectly normal in most respects, have struggled to find—and follow—their bliss against the lockstep pressures of "fitting in."

Comparing modern gardens to how we eat is a no-brainer. In just two or three generations we've gone from eating mostly home-cooked

Fast-food gardening means outsourcing most of our basic gardening pleasures.

food and gardening with mostly local resources to routine fast-food and "mow-and-blow" landscapes filled with unproductive, unsustainable plants from afar.

Similar to how "fast food" lured us away from plain home cooking, "fast-food gardening" has made it convenient to outsource most of our basic gardening pleasures.

Garden sizes have withered while waistlines have been supersized. Why bother to grow any of your own food when you can just run to the store and buy it, cheap and prepackaged? Instead of sowing saved seed, we buy uniform hybrids by the six-pack, grown and shipped to us at a huge cost (both economic and environmental). Sure, we've shed a lot of the menial work of putting both food on the table and flowers in the garden, but at what cost to the connections with the earth and our neighbors that our ancestors took for granted?

Slow Gardening has deep roots, because gardening has always been a process, a collaboration between humans and nature, and not something you can go out and buy. The passage of time is central: planting a little tree is just a beginning. A new plant—and it doesn't matter what you plant, as long as you plant something—gives you something new to check on and nurture, a new destination in your own garden, a new reason to keep an eye on the weather and to mark the passing seasons.

The Slow Gardening approach can help us enjoy our gardens year in and year out while connecting us with our neighbors.

By sharing gardening with garden "newbies" and especially children, we can actually help prepare others for a brighter, more sustainable future. In other words, through gardening with others, we can make the world a better place for future generations.

Children learn about the many wonders of life in the garden.

Some Slow Gardening Tenets

Gardening cannot be separated from its many intertwined concepts and activities.

Life is not a problem to be solved, but a reality to be experienced.
—Soren Kierkegaard

People often get bogged down with the details of life, seeing everything as a confusing morass of intricacies—like a ball of rubber bands.

This book attempts to "de-construct" gardening into simple acts that are in themselves only tools for attaining the bigger goal of savoring our lives. Here are a few of the basic concepts or tenets of Slow Gardening:

Take it easy. Slow doesn't necessarily mean simple or lazy. In fact, it can actually involve more work, just spread out over time in a leisurely fashion. It's a one-foot-in-front-of-the-other approach similar to preparing regular, interesting meals at home.

There is no need to get hung up about the rules of garden design and step-by-step instructions in gardening how-to books. You can be cussedly independent, contemplative, unhurried, and unworried. Be in it for the fun, and take your time about it.

Don't be paralyzed by what you're not doing right, or by what you think you ought to do. Slow Gardening does not discriminate based on materials, personal style, or level of interest or expertise.

Along these lines, Slow Gardening is less about style, and more a way of being in tune with whatever rings your bell. Slow Gardeners might be hard-core green gardeners with a penchant for native plants and sustainable methods, or sharply focused lawn fanatics, daylily collectors, or people who just love to grow tomatoes. They're not trying to get anywhere, since they have already reached their destination. If it thrills you and you're doing it, that's Slow Gardening.

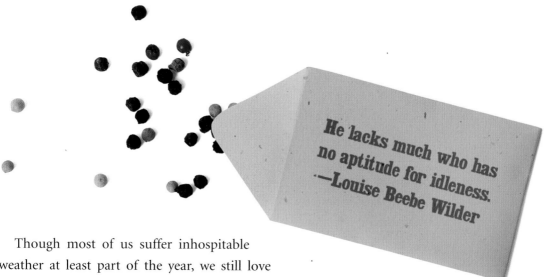

He lacks much who has no aptitude for idleness.
—Louise Beebe Wilder

Though most of us suffer inhospitable weather at least part of the year, we still love puttering around the yard and garden. So naturally, anything that connects us to our gardens without causing a lot of sweaty exertion is always welcome—especially if it is simple enough for the gardener to be the only moving part! Simple tools and simple motions, for simple pleasures.

Slow Gardeners don't mind spending more money trying to grow tomatoes than they'd have cost at the store, just for that first hot-off-the-vine bite in the summer.

And we grow plants of all descriptions that like our climate, and that provide something for local wildlife. We often grow attractive vegetables, fruits, and herbs that double as "regular" ornamentals in flower beds and pots.

We try to plan ahead so we can harvest food and flowers for as long as possible, with as little effort as practical. And we tend to seek out and plant heirloom vegetables, bulbs, and flowers that multiply readily so we can share with others.

Get 'er done. You don't have to be an expert to garden, or even to work very hard. Clichés can help:

Gardening enjoyment is an all-season affair.

No need to go whole hog right off the bat. Don't have to eat the whole enchilada.

In fact, your garden provides natural opportunities to kick back, relax, and step off the treadmill. Grab a digging fork or a water bucket, and slip right into the rhythm of the seasons.

Get together. Gardeners have always been a sharing tribe. Move into a new community that has gardeners, and it won't be long before someone chats you up (even in a grocery store line) about the weather or the season, which can quickly lead with a smile to something about gardening. Before you know it, your garden could have plants shared by seed, rooted cutting, or division, plus solid advice, all locally grown and region-specific.

None of this is new; this is how people have gardened for centuries, until the advent of television, air-conditioning, and the Internet drove us inside and away from neighbors.

But people want to get back to the garden—they just don't know how. When they turn to someone for help, they often get sidetracked by alluring advertisements, or lulled into having someone else do most, if not all, the work for them.

But there is a renewed interest in both community gardening and the all-important activity of gardening with children (both at school and at home). There are many horticultural societies, countless local garden clubs, and university master gardener groups. Most have regularly scheduled educational events, garden tours, and plant swaps and sales.

There are even "guerilla gardening" groups that work covertly to improve city life through public gardening, using fewer horticultural rules and more gardening know-how.

Passing along ideas and skills is easy in a garden setting.

There is no smile like a "homegrown" smile.

Slow Food, Slow Gardening—It's All Good

"A lot of people see Slow Food as a middle-class supper club," said Raj Patel, author of *Stuffed and Starved* and an expert in food security and justice issues. "But it was always Carlo Petrini's genius to see that the best way of recruiting people is through pleasure."

While Slow Gardening owes a lot to people who have learned to plan ahead to make sure good, nutritious homegrown food is available to themselves and their families, it is far more than just fruits, vegetables, and herbs and includes flowers, lawns, wildlife, and other garden enjoyments as well.

Still, the Slow Food folks have several important mantras that apply equally well to Slow Gardening, including growing and eating locally, eating in season, using sustainable practices, and sharing with others—particularly children.

All of which raises good questions for putting this into practice using a Slow Gardening approach.

To start with, why eat in season? There's a reason *locavore*—eating what is grown locally—was designated the 2007 Word of the Year by the folks who edit the venerable *Oxford English Dictionary*. If you are eating vegetables, fruits, and herbs close to the time of harvest, it means you are getting food at its peak of freshness. Though many foods can be stored for long periods (notably hard-rinded squash, potatoes, onions, and the like), the fresher it is, the tastier and more nutritious it is likely to be, and the fewer resources it has taken to store it or get it to you.

But Slow Gardening has lots of room for learning to "put up" food—drying herbs, making juices, jellies, and jams, storing hard-shell squash, and the like. It can be a point of pride to have home-

Farmers' markets provide locally grown produce in season.

grown food even in the middle of the winter, stored from your summer garden's harvest.

If you can't or don't want to grow it yourself, though, try to support local farmers. Eating locally, and eating what's in season, is easier when you shop at farmers' markets, farm stands, or outlets selling produce from other community-supported farms and community gardens; plus, spending your money locally at local farms also means you're helping to keep working farms viable, which helps lower transportation costs and ensures you will know who grows your food—and under what conditions. When you know the farmer personally, you can ask questions about how the produce was grown.

But there's no farm like your own, and, as they say, there's no food miles like *no* food miles. And the satisfactions and rewards of gardening—including health, benefits to wildlife, and achieving personal goals—go way beyond food, all of which will be dealt with in later chapters.

All these concepts—collectively called "green"—are age-old. People gardened this way long before anyone invented garden hoses, chemical fertilizers, or pesticides.

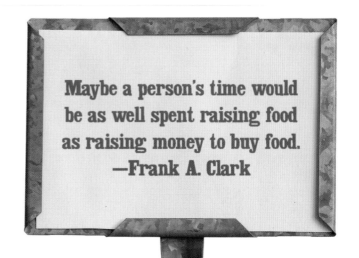

Maybe a person's time would be as well spent raising food as raising money to buy food.
—Frank A. Clark

Soft-Core Organic

Lastly, what's the big deal about organic gardening? Must we all toe the hard-core line?

Isn't there a little wiggle room for using reasonably safe modern synthetic materials, especially if it means the difference between having a crop to harvest and not having anything at all?

Sure there is, to most folks. But, just as numerous ancient cultures destroyed themselves using unsustainable practices, a lot of modern agriculture and gardening practices have been environmentally destructive by causing soil erosion, polluting water

Gardens provide habitats for many different forms of wildlife.

with fertilizers and chemical pesticides, and wiping out beneficial native wildlife. Not to mention the effects on our own health.

Some people tend to draw hard lines between chemical and organic gardening, but sometimes independent research simply doesn't support them all; in many cases the loudest proponents of one way over another have cherry-picked the facts to suit their own agenda.

It's like the debate over growing tomatoes versus eating canned ones. Though eating a tomato from a can and growing your own are vastly different experiences, the truth is, the nutritional value is very similar.

Still, organic growing methods are used by those who realize that the long-term health of the garden—especially the soil—depends on more than adding fertilizer and killing pests; it means taking care of what you have, even building it up. And there is no better way to accomplish this than through time-tested organic methods such as composting and using well-adapted plants.

The bottom line is, there is simply no reason to use chemicals reflexively, when so many great gardeners—even ones who aren't ideologically opposed to using them occasionally and sparingly—have found ways around them. We'll explore this more in chapter 5, "Nuts and Bolts."

Battle the Bulge

Have you ever felt like gardening is real work?

Let's face it, for most of us, gardening is a leisurely pursuit, with an occasional brisk chore worked in. But to get the recommended minimum amount of daily exercise, you'd have to do something fairly strenuous for half an hour at least five days a week—which is not likely in the heat of summer or cold of winter.

There are some pretty good activities: mowing the lawn, pruning shrubs, digging holes, turning compost, and raking leaves. But most of us get out of breath just hauling garbage to the street or putting bird feed out. Heck, in the humid summers where I live, I've sometimes worked up a soaking sweat just holding a water hose in my hand!

To get a little personal, not long ago I was in terrible shape—slightly obese, in fact. But when my son Ira left for Marine boot camp, I made a vow to lose weight. I changed my diet, switching from sugary to diet drinks (plus a lot more plain water), cutting back on the tamales and cornbread, eating more fruit as snacks, and simply pushing back from the table sooner than I used to.

And I started daily evening walks around the neighborhood, which took me past a lot of gardens, which in turn gave me a better appreciation of the diversity of plants and garden styles around me through all the seasons.

Gardening is about being outside and using your body as well as your mind.

Though I insisted all along that I wasn't trying to get healthy, just *less unhealthy*, the minor changes in my diet and moderate daily exercise helped me feel better physically, mentally, and even emotionally. And I lost thirty pounds and four inches off my waistline.

Now I feel more like doing stuff in the garden. Even small things involve stretching, bending, lifting, pushing, and pulling—all resistance exercises, without a lot of repetitive jarring and stress. I find that gardening also helps improve my attitude toward the minor vicissitudes (or sheer weirdness) of life.

Summing It Up

Slow Gardening is just good gardening, and it is good for you and your surroundings.

As I will cover in the next chapter, gardening has a lot to do with psychology and sociology—what and why we do stuff, and how we get along with neighbors. It culminates with my premise that good gardening takes a Gestalt approach—one that looks at the whole enchilada, not just the bits and pieces.

Slow Gardening is an attitude, not a "how-to" checklist of things to do or not do. No matter how you are wired for life, you can find ways to slow down enough to focus on what you are doing and to savor it.

This book will explore a good many ideas for helping you become more deliberate in your garden efforts, so you can use your mind, body, and spirit—and all your senses—for getting more from your life.

Gardens are also places of repose and relaxation.

Whether you are a home food grower, have the most intense interest in maintaining a perfect lawn, or just have a few potted plants indoors to keep you company and to help filter the indoor air, it makes sense to do it well, in a sustainable manner, and to share it with others so, collectively, we can help make a little difference in the world.

The Slow Gardening concept is very inclusive, with plenty of room for many different approaches that will work just fine for nearly anyone—make that *everyone*—regardless of personality or interests or abilities.

The more help a man has in his garden, the less it belongs to him. —William M. Davies

Keep foremost in your mind that a person with a nicer garden is not necessarily a better person; but if you *do* have a nice garden, it should be because you enjoy it, learn from it, eat from it, and share from it. And if, because of circumstances beyond your control, you find yourself having to hire someone else to dig or mow, do it yourself occasionally too, to be reminded of your intentions and to be connected with your garden.

The key to all this is that, if at all possible, *you do it yourself*, not outsourcing your pleasure by hiring it out to someone who does it merely for the money.

The following chapters deal with designing a garden space, general gardening practices, selecting appropriate plants, and ideas on practicing Slow Gardening. A lot of the information may be old hat to you, or so intrinsically common that it may come across as pedantic. However, it is important to see that Slow Gardening won't make you a perfect gardener; instead, it's a lifestyle-changing, one-step-at-a-time attitude, like losing weight.

The most important thing is that it be done willfully, purposefully, sustainably, and in a sharing sense. In the next chapter, we'll look at some basic psychology of what we do, and why, and how it applies to you as a gardener.

Unlike the other arts—architecture, painting, sculpture—that are judged by their immediate effect—gardening, like fine wine, require years for perfection. Nature's fourth dimension—growth—cannot be achieved except on her own schedule, which is beyond man's control.

—Ralph Griswold

CHAPTER TWO
Garden Psychology

Here are some rules for today:

- Don't sweat the small stuff.
- It's *all* small stuff.
- If you can't fix it, flee it, or fight it, flow with it.

Gardening is more than digging, planting, harvesting, and feeding birds. It has deep psychological pulls and thrusts that help get us up and outside and through the day.

We know that there are as many approaches to gardening as there are gardeners. How can we keep them from competing needlessly?

It helps to think through some pretty heavy psychology and sociology, involving what we think, why we garden the way we do, and how we can overcome initial reluctance to relax and garden easily—with fewer judgments about other gardeners who are, after all, just trying to do their own thing.

Why Good People Don't Garden

Every garden is a chore sometimes,
but no real garden is nothing but a chore.
    —Nancy Grasby

Let's start with the premise that not all people want to garden as much as we do. Truth is, the best-intentioned gardeners tend to look a little nutty to non-gardening neighbors—especially if the gardeners are exuberant or have an unusual approach or style.

That said, there are predictable reasons why good people who would love to garden don't. These reasons go way deeper than our merely having been raised on fast food and TV, and how surfing the Internet is more enjoyable than sweating out in the yard.

A lot of people see gardening as just a series of repetitive, mundane exercises, like Sisyphus endlessly rolling his rock up the mountainside, only to watch helplessly as it crashes back down to the bottom, then trudging back down to start rolling it up again.

It is far easier to just hire the work out to someone else, and stay inside where it's comfortable.

Some of these reasons not to garden are practical, starting with how so many folks are overworked or overstressed with other areas of their lives, including jobs, family, pets, and myriad other distractions, especially on nice weekends. After all, there are lots of other hobbies besides gardening!

Being pulled in many directions is enough stress in itself. Why, other than to save a little grocery money by growing stuff at home, should people take on the additional challenge of gardening? It's easier to

Only the mythical Sisyphus was doomed to eternal, repetitive toil.

JEAN PIAGET AND PLAY

While studying educational psychology, I was immersed in the teachings of Jean Piaget, who noted a distinct difference between cognitive and formal activities: the first involves what you do; the other, how you do it.

But what intrigued me the most was the concept of *assimilation*, or the ability to comprehend new experiences in such a way that you integrate them into your life, so they become part of who you are.

The beautiful thing about this is that when people "play"—which can be defined as "performing activities that have little or no regard to reality"—they are acting out fantasies. Because this helps people adjust to new concepts more easily, play is almost pure assimilation!

Gardening should be simple, enticing, and easy to share.

just mow the grass every couple of weeks and scurry back indoors.

And, in many parts of the country, the weather alone is daunting. It's either too hot or too cold, it's too dark after work, and the weather forecast is for more of the same.

Don't even mention the fear of what diseases mosquitoes might be carrying this year, let alone having to deal with spiders, bees, pollen, and the inevitable cuts and bruises that come from pruning and hauling garden stuff around. Staying indoors is far safer.

When bugs or diseases hit our plants, we are either too scared or too cheap or too lazy to figure out how to select and use an appropriate remedy; many pesticides are simply bad for us and the environment—or at least that is what we are told. Better not to risk anything at all than to lose it all.

On top of all that, there seem to be way too many rules for how to do even the simplest things, and we are afraid that if we do it wrong we will look stupid and risk the ridicule of neighbors.

It is easiest to simply not get started in the first place, or to give up quickly when the going gets rough.

So what to do? Well, if you are a new gardener, this book covers the basics in the most basic manner. If you are an experienced gardener, but have non-gardening friends, give those friends something simple to start with, something that has easy, obvious results, like a pot of hardy herbs, a handful of bulbs, or a cactus, with the gentle advice not to treat it kindly. Hook 'em with something small they can build on.

Hort vs. Sport

Gardening is the purest of human pleasures.
—Francis Bacon

A recent television commercial, meant to be lighthearted, featured well-known sports commentators dressed as garden experts comparing flowers, tongue-in-cheek. At the end the announcer says, "Aren't you glad they are into sports?"

As if gardening is an inferior pastime, and garden experts are less he-manly than sports experts. As Bugs Bunny would say, "Sheesh! What maroons!"

Do their mamas know they are making fun of gardeners this way?

I mean, Thomas Jefferson was a fantastic gardener. So was George Washington. And they were men's men, right? And I doubt anyone would suggest that Lady Chatterley's gardener-lover was lacking in any way other than social graces . . .

Here's a suggestion: turn football fields and golf courses over to gardeners for just one year.

Think about it. Slightly sloped fields, perfectly drained soils, irrigation already in place. There could be garden rows between the five-yard lines, and the concession stand could offer bottles of fertilizer alongside cold beverages, and seeds and perennials to go with the potato chips.

Gardening is not a competitive sport.

The track around the edge of the field could be a flea market for antique tools and wheelbarrows, and down in the end zone a tinker could set up shop for sharpening blades and adjusting small gas engines.

In the garden arena, we would encourage rather than fine our best players for using rooting hormones and growth enhancers. But then I guess we might have to banish those who overdo it with pesticides. And who needs cheerleaders, when we have garden gossips who tattle when someone growing hybrid tea roses sneaks out here at night to spray when nobody is looking . . .

Talk about a level playing field! Gardening doesn't require size or swiftness, so anyone can participate—even older folks with blown-out knees (perfect for aging sports stars turned commentators).

Don't expect to see *The Victory Garden* host's mug on a cereal box anytime soon. But here's wishing sports geeks would stop kicking sand in the eyes of hort-hunks.

Gardeners Anonymous

Gardening is a form of gambling, as I see it. Every time we sow a seed, we voluntarily participate in a risk-taking activity, an indulgent diversion that involves putting up an investment in time, money, supplies, and effort, hoping for a payout.

Me, I cheat. Who's to know if I don't follow the rules, in my own little garden casino? Sometimes I win, sometimes I lose. Sometimes I gamble that I won't drop dead from a heart attack digging in the humidity.

But the act of gardening is not a compulsion with me—I can stop anytime. Really. That is, unlike my lawn-mowing neighbors, most of whom are unwilling to admit they even have a problem; they think they have control of their habit, that they can stop all that endless mowing and plant lower-maintenance shrubs and ground covers and flowers like "real" gardeners.

Don't believe this is a problem? Then just look at how your garden controls your weekend. Better yet, ask yourself these questions, which could form the basis of a supportive Gardeners Anonymous (GardAnon) organization:

- Have you ever lost time from work (including in the house) to garden?
- Has spending more time in the garden ever made your home life unhappy?
- Does gardening affect your reputation (does the grocery store clerk know you garden)?
- Have you ever gardened with equipment that took money needed for other things?
- Do you think it's a perfect day just because the sun comes out after a good soaking rain?

SCHADENFREUDE HAPPENS

Ever see something slapstick that makes you suddenly laugh out loud, but you catch yourself because it isn't really funny to the person it happens to?

The Germans (and psychologists) call taking pleasure at someone else's misfortune *Schadenfreude*, and it happens to the best of us. It's chuckling when someone drops a basket of tomatoes or lightly whacks their head with a rake handle. It's secret glee when a disliked neighbor's lawn turns brown after being over-sprayed with weed killer.

This, like so many other emotions, is neither good nor bad, *it just is*. In the garden, as in the rest of life, schadenfreude happens.

Labels convey more than mere plant names.

- Is your lawn a place, not a chore?
- Can you smell when your compost has finished "cooking"?
- Did you ever garden longer than you had planned—or at night?
- Do you grow more than ten different varieties of any one plant?
- Do you have plant labels everywhere in the garden?
- Do you know how many bags of compost your car can hold, or have you ever cleaned your car with a leaf blower?
- Can you amuse yourself for an hour with a garden hose?
- Have you ever gardened to escape worry or trouble?

We know that no real compulsive gardener ever regains control on his own—with even just a small garden we tend to get worse, never better.

Fortunately there are steps you can take for a program of recovery. The first step is to concede fully to your innermost self that you are a compulsive gardener, to admit that you have lost the ability to control your habit. Admit that you are powerless, that a greater power is needed to help restore you to a normal way of thinking. Make amends to people your gardening habits have affected, and make an effort to carry this message to other compulsive gardening sufferers.

I can see the sweat popping out from your brow already, just thinking about your garden. Can you resist? *Can you just say no?*

The Gardener's Bill of Rights

Horticulture—the science and practice of crop production—has all sorts of rules and efficiency guidelines, and little room for doing stuff just for the love of it. Gardeners, on the other hand, often aren't in a hurry or looking for a payback other than the relaxation involved in growing stuff.

With that distinction in mind, I present this list of rights that are inalienable to all gardeners—few of which will make any sense at all to left-brained horticulturists, but all of which are good for the gardener's soul.

Therefore, be it hereafter known that a gardener shall have:

- The right to garden at any hour, day or night
- The right to plant stuff in the front yard, away from the house foundation
- The right to have no grass at all, except maybe a little patch upon which to lie on your back and watch the sky
- The right to plant any color of flower next to any other color of flower, even if they clash
- The right to cultivate plants others consider "weeds"
- The right to more potted plants than we can water
- The right to plant too many tomatoes every year
- The right to a leaf pile
- The right to as many wind chimes as we can afford—bird feeders, too
- The right to prune or *not* to prune leggy plants—with no questions asked
- The right to mispronounce plant names (and to use the *h* in "herbs")
- The right to wear big floppy hats and loose clothing—no matter how ridiculous we look

Amendment: The right to show our up-ended behinds to neighbors as we bend over digging and planting. Assuming, of course, that we are reasonably clothed.

Multiple Intelligences in the Garden

"The men where you live," said the little prince,
"raise 5,000 roses in the same garden—and they do
not find in it what they are looking for, and yet what
they are looking for could be found in one single rose,
or in a little water."
   And the little prince added: "But the eyes are blind.
One must look with the heart."
   —Antoine de Saint-Exupéry, *The Little Prince*

The "green thumb" is finally official.

When Harvard psychology professor Howard Gardner developed his theory of multiple intelligences, he noted that people possess several different types of intelligence and aptitude, in varying degrees. While everyone has a bit of each, some folks have more or less than their fair share of some.

The earliest innate intelligences Gardner uncovered were interpersonal (ability to work with groups); intrapersonal (independent work); kinesthetic (problem solving, don't need lots of directions); musical (rhythmic); and visual-spatial (artists, mappers, and the like). Linguistic and mathematical intelligences were also mapped.

I always felt that gardeners should be in there somewhere. Look around, and you'll see people who have an obvious *nurturing* intelligence; this would explain how the best gardeners, including those with no formal training in horticulture, can juggle and deal with the many ever-changing but long-term challenges of nature.

Then, to my delight, Gardner found evidence of an eighth intelligence with even its own special brain region that supports it: *naturalist*. People who are gifted with large dollops of naturalist intelligence can quickly recognize subtle distinctions in the natural world and easily relate everyday things to their environment. They gravitate toward natural phenomena.

Of course it's not just gardeners and farmers. Great hunters and fishermen (those who don't depend on a lot of high-tech gadgets), meteorologists, environmentalists, even cooks and others who observe and actually predict seemingly random changes in natural patterns, and act accordingly, are gifted with this ability.

John Muir had tons of it, as did Jacques Cousteau. So did Charles Darwin, and Rachel Carson. National garden guru Roger Swain has it in abundance.

Naturalists easily follow cyclic patterns such as seasons, tides, moon phases, and weather. They are very comfortable outdoors and automatically use their senses to explore their environment. They look around as they drive, watching weeds and hawks, and braking for butterflies.

They observe, touch, and compare even "yucky" things, and

often they collect stuff—shells, rocks, and flowers (often in mixed cottage gardens, or extensive collections of roses or daylilies or African violets).

They not only observe but also manipulate the environment to see if what happens can be predicted—ever-curious plant hybridizers fall heavily into the naturalist intelligence, as do "giant tomato" or "perfect lawn" gardeners. So do wildflower enthusiasts, bonsai artists, and garden teachers, whose naturalist leanings are coupled with strong interpersonal and linguistic abilities.

Does any of this apply to you? Mix in varying doses of the other intelligences, and we can see why gardeners have such different approaches, and levels of success and satisfaction.

So, it turns out, it's official—a green thumb is an innate intelligence that we're all born with, only some gardeners have more of it than others.

Maslow's Hierarchy of Needs

Homegrown herbs are one of the easiest ways to connect the garden with the table.

In the brilliant sunshine I felt the desire to take walks in muslin dresses completely soaked with my sweat, to stretch myself out in the grass without a thought, to take refuge in this sensual pleasure, in my body which doesn't need to depend on anybody.
—Simone de Beauvoir

No matter our interests or abilities, we often forget how easy it can be to find happiness and joy in gardening.

American psychologist Abraham Maslow theorized that until our lower, most base levels of needs are satisfied we will remain anxious and tense, unable to progress to or remain for long on higher levels.

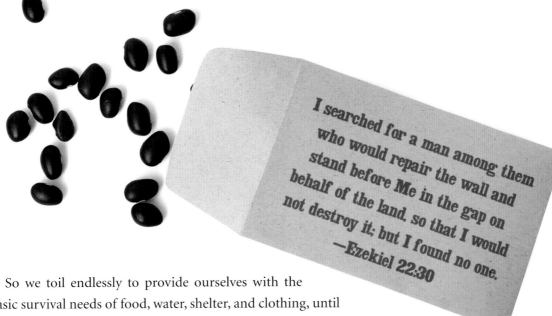

I searched for a man among them who would repair the wall and stand before Me in the gap on behalf of the land, so that I would not destroy it; but I found no one.
—Ezekiel 22:30

So we toil endlessly to provide ourselves with the basic survival needs of food, water, shelter, and clothing, until we manage to move up a tier by finding ways to provide a little security to make sure those needs will be met tomorrow and the next day. The yearning for a predictable, orderly life and world is the main reason why a lot of gardeners simply maintain what they have, in a metaphorical attempt to keep the wilderness at bay.

The third tier has to do with social needs: emotionally based relationships, social clubs, religious groups, sports teams, and so on. It is where we form friendships, find a supportive family, and find intimacy and love. This is where most gardeners get stuck, trying to "fit in" and be acceptable to our neighbors and society.

The fourth level is about finding esteem—the internal need to be respected, and to have self-respect. It's the very normal human need to feel like we are accepted and valued by others.

Even more intermediate levels of needs suggested by other researchers include "cognitive" needs, in which a person desires knowledge and understanding, and "aesthetic" needs, which include a need for beauty.

But the top level, according to Maslow, is called *self-actualization*, or the full realization of one's own maximum potential and possibilities. This is where we feel strongest, and able actually to do things that are not necessary to the other needs. When the other needs are satisfied, we are freed up to step outside the box, to embrace new realities, to be spontaneous and interested in solving problems.

This is where we are most able to accept ourselves and others without prejudice, and to develop a "philosophical" sense of humor that helps us resist outside pressures. It is where we are most likely to be independent enough to make changes in our environment rather than just cope with it.

This is the level at which Slow Gardening kicks in. It allows us to get beyond just planting, watering, harvesting, mowing, and all the other low-level activities that make up our work and gives us impetus to get out and help and encourage others, and to do little things that make the world a better place.

Transcendent Thinking

The one most intriguing—and rarely achieved—level of personal development—one not touched by Maslow's theory—is called *self-transcendence*. Usually sparked by a sudden or dramatic event such as a near-death experience, this level, often marked by humility and deep empathy for the misfortunes of others, is where the most divergent thinking occurs.

Transcendent gardeners are least likely to be bothered by fitting in, and more likely to advocate for change in society in order to help more individuals—or the world itself.

Slow Gardening: A Gestalt Approach

What is a garden, anyway?

For years I have hosted a radio program called *The Gestalt Gardener*. *Gestalt* is a German word used by psychologists to mean "form," "shape," or "configuration," as well as "the whole." The Gestalt approach, which has often been compared to Zen Buddhism and other Eastern philoso-

GARDEN EGALITARIANISM
LIFE, LIBERTY, AND THE PURSUIT
OF·HAPPINESS IN THE GARDEN

Egalitarianism is a philosophy that favors equality of some sort. It holds that plants, like gardeners, are equal in their inherent, fundamental worth. But while we can value all plants—starting with the apple used to kick us from the Garden of Eden—we recognize that there are different types of equality, or ways in which individual plants might be treated.

The same goes for garden styles, including naturalistic or "wild" gardens in otherwise "tame" neighborhoods.

Yet English philosopher John Locke espoused that each of us has the right to do whatever we choose with whatever we legitimately own, *so long as we do not violate the rights of others.*

So there may be limits on our rights, a prominent one being that every gardener has the duty to respect and ensure that the rights of every other gardener are protected—meaning you can't impose your garden style on your neighbors, any more than they should be able to impose theirs on you.

phies, provides an effective means of coping and enables us to assume more responsibility for our activities and life.

The emphasis is on what is being thought, felt, or done at the moment, rather than on what has happened in the past or what could or should be done later. The goal is to become aware of what you are doing and how you are doing it, while appreciating how it affects the whole.

The Gestalt concept is easily related to Slow Gardening by how it:

- uses an experiential, hands-on approach to gardening;
- takes into account the whole garden (or gardener—body, mind, and spirit);

- assesses what is happening in the present (the here-and-now);
- emphasizes self-awareness;
- encourages personal (garden) responsibility;
- acknowledges the integrity, sensitivity, and creativity of the gardener; and
- recognizes that the gardener is central to the gardening process.

Following these insights, a practicing Slow Gardener would be constantly aware of his or her place in the garden and, being an integral part of the process called gardening, would take responsibility for what does or does not happen.

This leads to some interesting insights. For example, as I look around my own little cottage garden, I see—at least in my mind's eye—an ever-evolving seasonal display of wildflowers. My neighbors, on the other hand, think that it's just a lot of weeds.

> Without deviation from the norm, progress is not possible.
> —Frank Zappa

Digging Deeper

Understanding a handful of other Gestalt principles can help us understand what we are doing—and why.

A garden is always in relation to human thought. More than a mere physical place, a garden is a concept of possibilities or potential. The gardener is free to choose among all possibilities from moment to moment. Through these choices one constructs a garden.

A garden can be found not in the details, but in the whole. The "left-brain" science of horticulture muddles us with details. Most folks get bogged down because further and finer analysis of what we are doing makes it more complicated—the closer we look, the more we find to see. A garden is much more than the summation of its parts; plants, structures, and all the other parts are mere background noise to the overall intention of the gardener.

Our previous experiences influence what we think and do. For the most part, gardeners are likely to stay in a comfort zone of what we already know or were taught. When we stray from that we set ourselves up for disappointment and criticism from others. Truth is, it doesn't matter what you do, or how you do it, people will talk about you anyway, so get over it, so you can move forward.

Lastly, *whimsy and humor are relief valves for the anxiety that comes from trying to do as we please.* Doing something a little odd—a bit of yard art, a funny way of pruning, an unusual lawn shape, whatever—gives a lift to the spirit while helping us feel better about not being in lockstep with everyone else.

Sharing starts with a single flower.

WORLDVIEW

What's your garden worldview—in other words, how do you see your garden and its place in the world?

Some gardeners prefer neatly organized landscapes, keeping everything clipped and coiffed to reflect control over their surroundings. As for people who conscientiously make up their bedroom even when nobody will ever see it, it gives them a sense of order, a grip on the rest of the day.

Others go for more relaxed cottage styles that seem cluttered and random to outsiders. Still others are involved with Zen-like mystical elements of Oriental gardens, or the sharing aspects of naturalistic gardens filled with wildlife.

If your choice of neighborhood doesn't reflect these various styles, you may end up having anxiety about what your neighbors think. And, along with taking daily doses of anxiety medication, you may choose to modify your garden to better fit with what is around you.

However, by adopting better gardening approaches—even in the face of criticism—you may actually influence folks around you to change their ways a little to reflect a better worldview.

There are as many kinds of gardens as there are gardeners.

The Gestalt approach—or, should I say, the Slow Gardening approach—helps us find common ground and peace between horticulture science and gardening just for the love of it. It includes ways to get more gardeners "into the fold" by relaxing—or even outright mocking—some of our cherished gardening rules, and it allows a garden to be seen as a whole, instead of a lot of details.

Slow Gardening isn't merely about growing your own food or saving the world. It's about doing what you savor, and savoring what you do. And when you savor things, you cherish them and usually want to share them with others. This puts gardeners in direct contact with other people, making possible social movement—where miraculous things can happen.

Which *can* help save the world.

In the following chapters we will get down to the business of gardening slow, with brief overviews on what to grow, where, and how, and ending with a serious checklist of Slow Gardening practices.

The author shares garden tips with students at the Slow Food University of Gastronomic Sciences in Italy.

CHAPTER THREE
Carving Out Your Space

Slow or not, no matter what our approach to gardening is, or what kinds of plants we choose, there must be a space to do it all in—a garden. If you don't feel like you are in a special place, an area where you feel secure enough to be yourself with family and friends, then something is terribly wrong.

The word *garden* comes from the Old English word *ghordos*, which meant a "guarded" area. The word also morphed into *courtyard* (same root word for *horticulture*), indicating an enclosed space; both assume a special place that is somehow protected, physically or otherwise, from the outside. A safe haven, so to speak.

In many cases, especially where space is tight or neighborhood restrictions are in place, this sense of being in a guarded area is easiest to pull off in the backyard, out of sight of the public.

But it doesn't take a high wall to create at least the feeling of enclosure; it can be attained by planting a low hedge, flower border, or a short section of fence that at least symbolically separates you from the street and neighbors. This feeling of being apart from others enables us to turn our garden into an oasis.

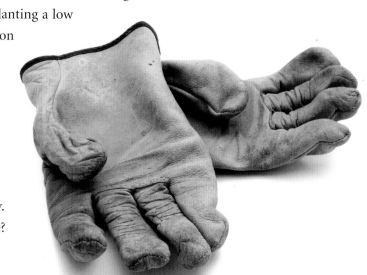

What is most important is the mental and emotional aspect of feeling secure, and free—of feeling okay. And, if not in the garden, then where?

A landscape should include all types of plants.

As I have written earlier, no matter what you do, or how you do it, your neighbors are going to talk about you anyway. So get over it and start gardening according to your own standards—this is the essence of Slow Gardening.

Landscape vs. Garden

So, do you have a garden or a landscape? It doesn't matter what you call it, but the difference does reflect how you approach what is outside your doors.

While the word *garden*—often shortened to *yard*—hints at an enclosed area, *landscape* generally means the whole property and typically includes the house with garage or toolshed, sitting areas (patios, decks), and other "hard" features (pool, arbor, fence, etc.), all connected with walks. The rest of the area—the default—has for decades now been mostly lawn (a term that hundreds of years ago simply meant an open glade or meadow), dotted with various combinations of plants.

Since the mid-1800s, most of our streets have shared an almost seamless lawn from one end to the other that maintained, at least visually, a democratic air of shared common values. We mow, we prune, and we expect our neighbors to do the same.

These functional, public landscapes rarely reflect differences among neighbors, to the extent that someone who doesn't maintain the prevailing standards will often be treated as a pariah, and sometimes even forced into compliance by city ordinance or neighborhood covenants. Self-expression is relegated to the backyard. Back there, highly personal gardens are typically enclosed areas designed from the house looking out, and filled with lots of plants of all kinds, including herbs and vegetables grown like flowers. For years these private garden spaces have been hidden out of public view.

These days, however, many people are lightening up on sterile and conforming public spaces. Just as formal front parlors and tidy "living" rooms, once used mostly for entertaining guests, have been transformed into all-purpose areas for entertaining family and friends, our front yards are starting to have more flowers and accessories for all the world to see.

The "New" American Garden Style

When people are free to do as they please,
they usually imitate each other.
  —Eric Hoffer

As I travel about, I see every imaginable approach to designing gardens: formal, classical, contemporary, Mediterranean, English, Japanese, cottage, naturalistic, whatever. They are all copies of something else, usually from another land or another time.

But the typical, fast-food American approach of having a row of gumdrop- and meatball-shaped shrubs hugging the foundation of the house—usually set there originally by building contractors—reminds me of a pig roast in which the cook tucks a little skirt of greenery around the baked ham. Parsley around the pig.

The typical foundation-style landscape is little more than an edging around a house.

But over the past two or three decades I've been noticing a new design aesthetic that's on the rise. This new approach to big spaces is especially striking in older neighborhoods where middle-aged "baby boomers" have settled, and where people care what others think but are still expressive—not copycats like our grandparents' generation.

It's a practical way of settling down, away from the high maintenance we were raised with. It starts with planting hardy flowers and shrubs away from the foundation, out by the mailbox or along the street, or partway up the side of the yard, and under mature trees where grass has finally petered out.

It involves making a subtle change in our typical landscapes, proving to neighbors that it can be done without society crumbling down. And with a lot less mowing.

I'm not talking about a "cottage garden" style, which is the exact opposite of the familiar manicured "suburban" style we were raised with (wall-to-wall lawn, a pair of trees, gumdrop-shaped shrubs hugging the foundation). Cottage gardens, though perfectly acceptable with their fences and arbors, their "one of everything" assortment of plants, their generous paths of mulch, flagstone, or crushed rock, and practically no lawn, are not for everyone. They take skill and time.

Instead, what I'm seeing is a steady shift toward a *modified* suburban style—what the American Horticultural Society calls the New American style.

In 1986, I attended the opening of the "New American Garden" demonstration at the National Arboretum near Washington, D.C.; instead of wall-to-wall grass and pruned shrubs hugging the house, it had a smaller but well-defined lawn surrounded with large mulched beds of small trees out near the street, with mixed shrubs, ornamental grasses, super-durable perennials, and a few masses of annuals to punch up the color and act as "bridges" between seasons.

Unlike traditional cottage gardens, the New American style usually has no fence and is best viewed from the street rather than from the house. With its year-round color and texture and low maintenance, it is often used by fast-food restaurants.

Its components make sense: Less than half the front yard is lawn, set off by generous, easy-to-mow-around beds of mulch or ground covers. In the beds are naturalistic groups of hardy trees underplanted with tough shrubs, fronted with repeated, bold groups of just a few tough perennials and ornamental grasses, with a few annuals here and there to visually tie it all together.

Regardless of climate region and which specific plants are used in the design, this style is now creeping into all neighborhoods, especially where folks don't really care what it's called. They're embracing colorful, lower-maintenance gardens that aren't the cookie-cutter "mow-and-blow" designs of our parents.

This style works well, and it

The New American Garden style has a reduced lawn with exaggerated other features.

Liminality—Garden Thresholds

As my garden slowly becomes a very private space for my muse, I sometimes find myself getting a little indecisive about what to do, which direction to go in. I end up betwixt and between different states of mind, as if I'm suspended in limbo, the twilight zone of being neither here nor there.

This state of mind is called *liminality*, after the Latin word *limen*, which literally means "doorway" or "threshold" and implies a transition of sorts. It's like both puberty and retirement, periods of neither this nor that during which normal thoughts are both agitated and relaxed, which can lead to new perspectives.

British cultural anthropologist Victor Turner coined the term *liminoid* to refer to experiences that are not quite thresholds (as in a graduation ceremony), but more "suspended" breaks from routine—like reading a book or going to a concert.

Or like gardening, where, unless you are simply mowing the lawn to maintain good relations with the neighbors, or tending a vegetable plot for filling the freezer, you are usually "puttering" around and doing stuff that has little to do with the reality of your life. Gardening usually isn't forward-moving production; it doesn't get the dishes washed, bills paid, or errands run.

It's a state of suspension, of relaxation. Of slowing down for a bit and paying attention to something out of the ordinary slate of daily chores.

> The garden reconciles human art and wild nature, hard work and deep pleasure, spiritual practice and the material world. ... It has its own liminality, its point of balance between great extremes.
>
> —Thomas Moore

allows folks to have more interesting landscape gardens that still look "normal."

And, by the way, most neighbors, while at first a little shy about embracing sudden changes, slowly adapt as bold, more experienced gardeners try new things. Often there is someone down the street just waiting for someone—perhaps yourself—to make the first move with this solid gardening trend.

Landscaping Made Easy

Designing for Slow Gardening, while rewarding both in the day-to-day activities and over the long haul, takes a little time and effort to get started.

A lot of gardeners—particularly new gardeners, or folks in new homes—feel overwhelmed by the blank canvas of a new garden. What to do? Where to start? How long will it take? With endless possibilities before us, these questions can all but paralyze us.

But, as J. R. R. Tolkein wrote in *The Hobbit*, "the longest roads begin with the first step." Making that first footprint—perhaps by simply putting something, *almost anything*, out in the garden where you can see it from indoors—is a start. Could be a sculpture, or a bird feeder, or an architectural plant with strong lines or color.

Then, if you make a path or walk to the focal point, your garden will be divided into "this side" and "that side" and you can start planting one or the other.

I know this smacks of recipe gardening, but once that something special is out there, your eye and your mind won't leave it alone; soon other items and plants will follow, and you're on your way!

Unless you choose to live in a gated community with strict rules and covenants—in which case you will need to hide gardening passions behind a fence in the backyard—no one should be allowed to tell you what to do in your own private Eden. And these days, there is no real need to toe the line and do what everyone else is doing, especially if that means spending your precious life pushing around noisy mowers and string trimmers (or outsourcing this job to professional "mow-and-blow" landscape-maintenance companies) just to please the neighborhood.

A lawn can be made more interesting with a practical walk.

Because of ever-tightening restrictions on water, fertilizer, and pesticide use, and less time to play on a large expanse of turfgrass, there are several very clear trends in many areas toward smaller lawns, more ground covers and mulches, groups and masses of lower-maintenance shrubs and trees (especially well-adapted natives), fewer pesticides, and less noise and pollution from power equipment. Less time spent doing chores means more time relaxing and enjoying an easier life.

Of course, this is the way gardening has been done for decades in small communities across the world where most people are simply too busy with the essentials of living to waste much effort in trying to impress their neighbors with garden finesse.

Edging for a Neater Garden

A garden edge, whether a straight line or gentle curve, is more than a mere one-dimensional line separating (or joining) contrasting areas. More than where the patio or sidewalk and flower bed meet, or where the grass disappears into the shade. More than a fence or hedge, or the shore of a pond.

More specifically, whether it creates a sense of enclosure or dramatically defines two spaces, an edge is an opportunity. It can be a soft, unobtrusive transition, such as a slight change in elevation, or when two neighbors have different kinds of grasses or mowing heights. Or it can be a hard, precise architectural element like a fence, or a row of trees or shrubs, or a long, narrow flower bed between neighbors, or between the front yard and the back.

Neat edges make a lawn shine like a gem.

TRICKS OF THE LANDSCAPING TRADE

For folks who want to have a nice-looking garden filled with easy-to-grow plants, and who want to go slow in their day-to-day work, here are a few tricks to getting more use out of your garden with less effort:

- When creating a lawn, think backward: instead of carving flower and shrub beds out of the larger lawn area, make the lawn itself the dominant shape, which creates a bolder, stronger effect and helps reduce tight mowing corners.
- Use mulches and ground covers to reduce the amount of turfgrass, especially in areas that are hard to mow; both require less maintenance than turfgrass. Remember, when it comes to mulch as a landscape design element, browns are colors, too.
- It's fine to plant around the foundation of the house, but there is no need for a hard-to-keep-pruned green moustache of little gumdrop shrubs all the way across the front. Plant a nice combination of plants near the entrance as a focal point, and some bushes at corners, and let the rest look fine as just clean architectural lines.
- Plant from your own point of view. There's no need to put on a show that can only be seen from the street.
- Lose any plants that are killing you with maintenance. If a plant needs regular pruning or spraying, yank it out and put in its place some-

The lawn can be designed to be the dominant shape of the garden.

Experienced flower gardeners often dig shallow ditches, called *Victorian edges*, between lawns and flower beds; they are easy to keep clean, neat, and weed-free. The cut is made on the lawn side, with the ditch sloped up toward the flower bed. This makes it easier to maintain and provides a crisper edge.

More permanent edging material not only helps define the space

thing else that does what you want it to naturally.

- Connect plants into larger beds with mulches or ground covers, and plant trees in small groups rather than as individuals to be mowed around. Keep in mind that curves have fewer corners to deal with when mowing.
- Flat is boring. Add a small dirt pile to provide some elevation, call it a "berm," and plant it with low-growing perennials.
- Go vertical to take your eyes off the ground: put up an arbor, or at least a gate, and plant vines and hang potted baskets.
- Cluster plants with high water needs close together to avoid having to drag hoses everywhere.
- Give yourself something to look at. Stop staring out the window at a bare back fence or hedge by putting something out there to see: a bird feeder, pretty plants, garden sculpture (have fun!), a water feature, a smiley face on the fence, even a mirror—*whatever*. Just don't stare at your neighbors staring back at you.

- Make a comfortable place to sit—or even dine—outside. Make sure seating areas stay dry after rains, cool in the summer, and out of the cold winter winds. Include a fan where mosquitoes can be bothersome.
- Add any or all of these elements: soothing evening lighting; a water feature for background noise; fragrant plants (especially ones with scent in the evening, when you are most likely to be outside); wind chimes; and outdoor speakers for enjoying music.

Where possible, a garden should have comfortable seating throughout all seasons.

better but also clearly creates a visual effect. And it can also hold soil in a raised bed in place. Good materials for hard edging include bricks—regular or decorative ceramic—or naturalistic flagstone; softer-looking wood (using the newer, safer forms of pressure-treated wood and wood/plastic products for longer-lasting effect) that can be painted or stained for added color to the garden; vine-woven cottage-garden "wattle" fencing; or even whimsical recycled materials such as old kitchen plates or wine bottles stuck neck-down in the ground.

An edge works not only as a functional design element and as a practical border for raised beds; it also says something about the garden—and the gardener.

Landscaping for Winter Interest

In seed time learn, in harvest teach, in winter enjoy.
—William Blake

My garden, so color-drenched and lush with foliage in the summer, seems more bare than I can bear in the winter. The details normally hidden or toned down in warm seasons—walks, border materials, mulches, and edges of decks—are exposed, and the garden art pieces, usually seen only one at a time, are visible in excess, and they vie with one another for attention. It's downright distracting, even to me.

The garden needs something to tie the junky aspects together visually, to create focal points that draw the eye from point to point as opposed to the mishmash "kaleidoscope" effect.

Taking the advice of a landscape designer, I repeated groups of small evergreen shrubs here and there, with no real rhyme or reason, just wherever I thought the garden needed some "bones."

And BAM! It worked. Instantly. Not only do they make little dark green punctuation marks around the garden, but they also lend contrasting shape and color to the other plants.

Here are some other things you can do to create winter interest in your garden:

- Make sure weeds and frost-damaged perennials (ferns, lantana, cannas, etc.) are cut and composted, the lawn edged, and the garden raked free of leaf clutter. Clean up the garden, remove stakes, and generally neaten stuff up.

Design a garden for all-season interest and use.

Winter is more interesting with small details.

• In regions with mild winters, replace summer annuals with cold-hardy annuals such as pansies (*Viola*), sweet William, ornamental cabbage and kale, snapdragons, and even colorful winter salad greens. Position perennials with winter foliage for best effect, including yarrow, iris, and dianthus.

• Add interesting shrubs and small trees for winter texture, color, berries, and trunk forms; break up lines of shrubs and long fences with plants having contrasting leaf shapes and foliage color.

• In warm-winter areas, add winter-flowering shrubs such as camellia, winter honeysuckle, flowering quince, mahonia, spirea, flowering almond, or witch hazel.

• Place a "hard feature" in the landscape, such as a large rock, bird bath, sculpture, urn, or trellis, gate, or small section of fence (wrought iron, picket—whatever suits your style).

• Enlarge small plantings by working up the soil in a wide curve or other shape, and cover with mulch (pine straw or shredded bark), which gives instant good looks until you get around to planting more. Add a few sections of mulch and edging material such as brick, rock, or even broken pottery, for extra definition.

• Plant spring-blooming bulbs, hollyhocks, parsley, and other perennials (bought, or divided from your own garden) early, so they can get settled in before winter and perform much better in spring.

- Overstuff a large pot on a sunny porch with several kinds of cold-hardy plants, including winter annuals, bulbs, cascading ground covers, small "texturey" shrubs, etc. Group several kinds of indoor potted plants together near a window for a tropical touch (and also to help them cope with low humidity indoors).
- Set up a simple platform-type bird-feeding station to attract this most colorful addition to the winter landscape. Stock with black-oil sunflower seed.
- Install and position low-voltage night lighting to illuminate steps without blinding visitors as they enter and leave your home late at night.

Garden Structures and Hard Features

The beautiful rests on the foundations of the necessary.
—Ralph Waldo Emerson

Just as well-dressed people know how the right tie or brooch can draw attention, creating a strong focal point near the entrance to your home

WHAT MAKES A GOOD SWING?

My covered arbor is angled so it shields me and my guests from the hot afternoon sun from one side but catches and funnels our few summer breezes from the other.

It was fast and easy to build, and it demands a *lot* less maintenance than shrubs or trees. And it was made really tall on purpose, so I could use extra-long chains for my porch swings. A moving seat is not only relaxing but also helps keep biting insects off target.

To get the very most out of a relaxing porch or garden swing, remember this: the longer the chain, the slower the swing.

Create a welcoming entry to the garden.

can draw attention away from even the most ordinary architecture or landscape. Even something as simple as painting your door, installing a showy porch light, or planting a single large container or urn (or a matching pair) can be effective.

A garden simply would not be a garden without the "hard" features that encompass and define it and help make it work. Walks, decks, seating, walls, arbors, toolsheds, greenhouses, compost bins, raised beds and pots, and even bird feeders, water features, and fire pits are all part of what helps us use—and enjoy—the space we call our garden.

To create a feeling of enclosure and security—the essence of a garden—there should be something separating you from neighbors or the wilderness. Where shrub hedging may take years to fill in, fences and gates are instant solutions. They can be made of nearly any material, from wood (solid or woven) to metal or brick, which determines looks, cost, and longevity. In many cases a combination of fencing and shrubs or evergreen trees can be effective; in fact, shrubs and vines can be used to "tone down" solid walls.

Fencing also has practical uses, not the least of which is keeping out unwanted traffic—especially people (including neighborhood kids, if you have a pool or other attractive but dangerous water feature) and deer. Effective deer fencing should be *at least* six or seven feet high.

Gates should be sturdy enough to withstand constant use and can be creatively designed to add interest and style to the entire garden.

Arbors and pillars provide all-important "vertical" effects, which help keep your eyes off the ground, as well as being perfect for creating shade, especially when covered in vines. They do not have to be complex in

A rose pillar or arbor provides a strong vertical interest.

construction; a bold arbor made of fewer, larger, sturdier posts usually works well without needing a lot of upkeep—and it is an almost instant addition, compared with trees and large shrubs that take years to grow tall.

A small, ranch-style house with the traditional foundation-style land-scape (shrubs hugging the house foundation) can be quickly spruced up with an arbor put over the front entry. This simple addition can provide an instant (and inexpensive) detail that both softens the lines of the house and makes the entire landscape stand out.

A simple arbor or gate with some shrubs on either side can also be installed on the side of the house to separate the front yard from the back. Even without a solid fence it creates interest and a suggestion of mystery.

The keys to all these simple "retrofit" design elements are boldness and simplicity.

Without garden walkways, where would you put your feet? This seemingly dumb question is surprisingly overlooked by many gardeners. It isn't enough to get from the street to your doorstep; what about getting around the side of the house, or out to the toolshed, or to the corners of your garden? Without walks, you would have to walk on what—the grass? Dirt?

Walkways connect the dots in the garden. To move freely during all seasons without tracking hot dust or wet mud into the house and to get up slopes without worrying about slipping (especially when carrying stuff or at night) are precious conveniences.

To be practical, walks are normally as direct as possible, and they should be at least two feet wide without distracting interruptions (stepping-stones require more attention than you may always have). A three-foot width is more prac-

An arbor creates entrances between garden spaces.

BAFFLE THE NEIGHBORS

One of the most overlooked devices for creating privacy or screening out bad views is called a "baffle"— a section of fence or lattice that is raised up off the ground a little, like a small advertising billboard a few feet high and a few feet off the ground. Think "hand-shading your eyes from the sun" and you get the general idea.

Baffles can be small or large, vertical or horizontal, and, when placed close to the house or outdoor seating area, they can easily hide larger distant views without cutting off cool airflows. Individual baffles can be built and repeated as needed to get good screening without being too distracting.

Baffles made of lattice can be further toned down with vines, while solid baffles can be painted or stained, or decorated with wall hangings.

Simple baffles can hide as much in tight spaces as a larger garden wall.

tical, but it takes at least a four-foot-wide path for two adults to walk comfortably side by side.

Walks can be paved with concrete, brick, or flagstone; they can be filled with crushed stone packed down to an even consistency or even hard-packed dirt with a little concrete mixed in for firmness. Loose gravel is often hard to walk on, noisy, and prone to getting filled with debris. Paths of soft natural mulches are practical in extended woodland settings, especially when lined with fallen branches or other materials to keep them defined and easier to maintain.

LIGHTING THE WAY

Night lighting not only makes walking safer, but it also encourages people to take an evening stroll—especially when it's hidden from view so that no light shines directly into the eyes of visitors (including when they step off your porch, perhaps after having a glass of wine).

Low-voltage night-lighting is very easy to install by simply attaching a weather-proof transformer (similar to what runs toy electric trains) to an outdoor electrical outlet, then running special wires around the garden and attaching individual light fixtures where needed. Arrange the fixtures to shine on plants and walks, not in your eyes. Set the timer on the transformer to come on right before dusk and to go off later in the evening or by morning.

Any time you use electricity in the garden—even low-voltage night light-ing—it's important to prevent acci-dental shock by installing a ground fault circuit interrupter, similar to what is found in bathrooms near water—unless you use solar-powered stick lights (which are not very bright and require sunny days to work later at night).

Night lighting can be attractive as well as functional.

Gathering places such as porches, patios, and decks help get people outside, especially if they are large enough for people to move around easily and are protected from weather. Provide shade for summer sun, screening (walls or hedges) for cold winter winds, and an arbor or roof for rainy weather. Make sure steps are clearly marked or lighted.

Outdoor furniture should be comfortable to use, weatherproof, and easy to clean. It should be placed so it stays dry in wet weather and cool to the touch in hot weather.

Work areas and toolsheds should be easily accessible and at least theoretically free of clutter, with special storage places for fuel, pesticides, and other flammable or dangerous materials.

While it's true that "a messy desk is a sign of a busy person," if outbuildings and other structures are meant to be seen as part of the overall garden scene, try to make them blend in with the rest of the garden; borrow trim or paint colors from your home. Remember: a garden represents the gardener.

A greenhouse can be either freestanding or built as a "lean-to" against another structure, which saves both building costs and energy. To work well, site the greenhouse where it will get maximum sun exposure, especially in the winter (it can be shaded in the summer), and where it will be protected on the north side from cold winter winds. To keep your feet dry while watering plants in the greenhouse, make sure you stand on something firm, such as concrete paving blocks or a slightly sloped concrete floor that allows water to run off.

While formal compost bins are not required for making compost, the recycling area of the garden can be a source of pride—even entertainment for visitors, if it looks inviting enough. Some gardeners may prefer an informal, messy look, as if the area is used a lot; on the other hand, a neat, orderly area can be more efficient as well as attractive. For more tips on composting, see chapter 5.

Bird feeders, water features, and bird and bat houses help encourage a good balance of wildlife in the garden. They can be of any style and made of nearly any material and always lend attractive visual accents.

Other add-on elements for gardens include wind chimes (carefully selected for their specific tones), flags and pennants for color and motion, wall ornaments

Garden structures can provide instant shade, especially when covered with fast-growing vining plants like these ornamental gourds.

Even a toolshed can become a garden with a planted green roof.

GREEN ROOFS

Any small structure with a sturdy roof can have plants on top, which will help cool the structure in the summer, insulate it in the winter, and slow rainfall runoff all year round. Such "green roofs" can be either practical or attractive—or both.

Cover the roof with a waterproof material, install small terraces to keep soil and plants from sliding off, and fill with a lightweight soil mix. Gutters can collect water runoff and direct it either to the garden or to storage barrels for later use.

Add small plants that spread naturally, mat together, and are evergreen for all-season effect. Hardy succulents, grasses, ground covers, and small bulbs usually work well, but they may need watering during extreme dry spells. Also, be prepared to get atop the roof to weed from time to time.

(including mirrors for brightening dark areas—good *feng shui* [see page 59]—and appearing to increase the size of the garden), and decorative finials—formal, whimsical, or contemporary—to top fence posts.

In fact, garden art is one of the easiest ways to add interest, color, texture, and style to a garden. Whether it is a classical statue or a folksy scarecrow, an antique cast-iron heron or concrete chicken (or pink flamingo), a reflective glass orb or colorful "bottle" tree, a Japanese lantern or contemporary sculpture, a big piece of driftwood or a simple, bold urn, anything you add that creates a focal point lends its attitude to your entire garden.

It's your garden, your space. Personalize it with garden art and other embellishments.

Gardening in Containers and Raised Beds

Plants overstuffed into large containers make for instant eye appeal and, except for their increased watering needs, are much easier to care for than in-ground plantings. The containers themselves draw attention and add pizzazz to their garden settings.

Whether they are made of clay, metal, plastic, or other durable material, containers serve as perfect vessels for flowers, herbs, vegetables, and even small fruit plants, and they can be set where they get the best light. A combination of different-size containers often makes more of a visual impact, but keep in mind that small pots require more watering and are more likely to tip over in windy weather than larger pots. Also, you can put several plants in one large pot for an interesting arrangement that includes seasonal as well as year-round interest.

Any garden row or flower bed that has been widened and made more or less permanent is a raised bed. Raised beds are typically three to four feet across and raised up a foot or so; many gardeners reinforce the sides with wood, stones, bricks, or other material, but this isn't necessary.

Raised beds can be planted as needed, usually with hand tools or a small tiller, rather than having to wait until the entire garden has been harvested or is ready to be tilled. They drain well during spells of heavy rain and warm up early in the spring; however, they must be watered more often than standard garden rows.

Rather than simply placing raised beds on top of the existing soil—which essentially turns them into large container gardens in need of constant watering—it is better to have the beds partly sunk, to help reduce watering needs in dry spells. Raised beds usually have native soils dug several inches

Container gardens add interest as well as practical planting places.

Some climates are too arid for raised beds, making sunken beds more practical.

Raised beds make the most of small spaces and make gardening easier.

deep, and amended with organic materials such as peat moss, compost, manure, finely ground bark, etc.; because they are partly raised and partly sunk, they usually provide fifteen or more inches of root area, more than enough for most plants.

My best rule of thumb for how much organic matter to add is this: to a shovel's depth of native soil, add three to four inches of organic matter; it's best to use a little each of two or three kinds of materials such as compost, bark, manure, or potting soil, rather than a lot of what is just the cheapest. This ratio makes for better root growth with less watering than a completely artificial soil mix would need.

Raised beds—like flower beds—can be planted intensely, with irregular spacing and interplanting of several different kinds of vegetables, herbs, and flowers. Choose companion plants that have similar cultural requirements (watering, feeding, spraying) and that are productive in small spaces.

Feng Shui Is Not a Nasty Word

Meandering leads to perfection.
—Lao Tzu

The idea that a garden should be comfortable, soothing, relaxing, and otherwise good-feeling is nothing new, but unfortunately too many gardeners have exactly the opposite experience.

Enter *feng shui* (pronounced "fung-shway")! This ancient design concept is not a religion and doesn't have to be complicated; it's simply a few concepts and easy principles employed to create a pleasing, harmonious design, coupling common sense and the art of good placement. It works with, not against, nature and takes into consideration many different elements. Though no two gardeners use the same "recipe," here are a few basic principles to consider.

If you can assume that there are universal energies flowing around us at all times, feng shui (which means the flow of "wind" and "water") tries to attract that which is good and minimize that which is bad, to balance passive and active qualities (yin and yang), and to create a positive, happy relationship between us, our home, and the environment.

GODWOTTERY

I finally found a word to describe my cluttered cottage garden: *godwottery*.

Right before I began a garden club lecture, the ladies chanted a poem by Thomas Edward Brown (1830-97) in which, to describe his cluttered garden, the poet used a term chosen to rhyme with a line ending in "rose plot." The line is "A garden is a lovesome thing, God wot!"

Wot is an archaic term that means "to know," so it made sense to Brown. But since then, the word *godwottery* has come to mean, in addition to super-flowery language, an exaggeratedly elaborate garden that contains a wild assortment of plants and objects.

And isn't that what my garden is? Formal shrubs pruned into little meatballs toning down messy wildflowers, vegetables, and herbs grown in flower beds; a tiny lawn growing in a little red wagon; flower-filled tires, gnomes and flamingos, windmills, bottle trees; an iron fire pit beside a splashy artificial waterfall; a mannequin watching over it all . . .

Some folks don't care for this aesthetic. But many do, with at least a small slice of godwottery tucked in somewhere. And it's a good thing, God wot!

Whimsical homemade garden art can brighten any garden.

The five elements or forces (wood, fire, earth, metal, water) can be arranged in a natural or productive cycle. Examples of each element include live plants, an outdoor fireplace (or a grouping of red- and yellow-colored plants), terra cotta pots or other clay statuary, large stones, a water feature of any type, and metal sculptures or wind chimes. Try to balance these elements in terms of their size and placement so that none is more dominant than the others.

Also, we can redesign or modify unnatural or "unhappy" elements of design, such as excessive straight lines, sharp angles, narrow walks and steps, poor lighting, clutter, violently clashing colors, competing sounds, bad weather exposure, poor plant choices, and so on, to improve the overall feel of our garden.

While feng shui experts strongly dislike "recipes" for bringing calm into the garden, here are a few easy—and universal—concepts you can work into your garden:

- Remove clutter and dead plants to give a positive feeling to the entire garden space.
- Create a roomy space for people to gather and relax—a deck, patio, or small lawn area.
- Place garden furniture where you can have your back to a wall or hedge, with an unobstructed view of the garden; have small tables, plants (including ones in pots), or even large boulders to one side like arms on an armchair. Add a footstool for putting up your feet. In other words, make your guests and yourself comfortable and feeling safe and secure.
- Place a strong visual element—a low plant grouping, water feature, fire pit, etc.—in the near center of the garden, like a coffee table in a room.
- Remove straight linear walks or redesign them into gentle curves, or place a plant, urn, sculpture, or other impediment to break up straight lines.
- Tone down corners and edges with plants or garden art. Whenever possible, choose rounded art forms over pointed ones.
- Use subdued colors that blend together rather than clash loudly.
- Brighten dark areas and dispel gloom, especially in corners, by adding lights, mirrors, or light-colored plants.
- Include a clear pond to reflect the sky, and perhaps a waterfall with its soothing sounds.
- Avoid having good energy leading away from the home or from a viewing area by placing water features so that any moving water flows toward the house and viewing area, or at least passes to one side.

Curved walks create interest and soften lines.

- Include a gentle wind chime to soothe the spirit and mind, and ornamental grasses to capture and bring to life passing breezes.
- Choose plants that please you, not high-maintenance types that irritate you with their demands, and plant them where they will grow best—plants that grow in good light and good soil give off positive feelings.
- Arrange plants so they are mixed in different sizes, shapes, and colors, so no single one will be overwhelmed by the others.

These are not "rules" for feng shui, merely general principles and concepts; while it is not critical to include them all, a good garden will usually have them anyway. The important thing is to slowly transform your garden by gradually replacing those things (plants as well as design features) that bother or irritate you with those that help you feel more comfortable and relaxed.

Now *that* would be good feng shui!

Putting It All Together

Landscape, garden, whatever—it's your space, and you should look forward to being in it and relaxed, not feeling overwhelmed by chores.

The best way to reach this lofty overall goal is to have a good idea of what you want, then design or redesign accordingly. Most good landscapes include hard features such as walls, walks, sitting areas, and work areas; a pleasing mix of easy-to-care-for plants that do everything you want (good looks, good challenges, or good eats) without adding to your workload; and all the little niceties that help make you want to go outside and stay there as long as possible—even into the evening.

A great garden will include something to appeal to all your senses, all year-round, plus something for wildlife and a few aesthetic or artsy items just to tickle your fancy.

The garden, in other words, should be "whole hog"—not just something that's pretty to look at from a window, or from the street.

QUICK GARDEN FIX-UP

You've seen movie comedies where someone untidy has unexpected visitors and quickly stuffs pizza boxes under pillows, throws drink cans behind the couch, and puts unwashed dishes in the oven? Same thing happens when garden slackers like me have company.

When horticulture friends swing by my cluttered cottage garden unexpectedly, they expect to see the same garden that has been featured in magazine photos. But believe me, camera angles can make even the worst pig's ear look like a silk purse.

Luckily, these folks know that I don't subscribe to the coiffed, "blow-dried" landscape approach—too high maintenance for me; I went with a cottage garden style that is *supposed* to be unruly.

Still, I want to show my garden to its best advantage. Translation: Pull weeds, empty dead plants from pots, and compost my mistakes.

I pick up errant plastic pots, gather odd pieces of wood and fallen twigs, and rework my compost pile (which usually needs turning anyway). I empty green slimy water from my rain gauges, smooth out areas in my flower beds that our cats use as outdoor potties, and throw mulch over bare spots.

I edge my walks with a string trimmer and sweep leaves and bird seed hulls off the decks. I hose everything down to settle the dust and make stuff sparkle.

After this fast and furious work I always feel better, because it all needed doing anyway. But every time I do this, I remind myself that the Slow approach would have been to do it all along, a little at a time.

Can We Learn to Get Along?

They who are all things to their neighbors
cease to be anything to themselves.
—Norman Douglas

It's funny how most gardeners are convinced to their bones that, down deep, everyone else either thinks the same way they do or should just come to their senses.

Problem is, most folks don't share exactly the same perspective. Because of our unique combinations of experiences, values, education, observations, and the like, each of us has a different worldview that largely determines what we believe is right or wrong. And this definitely spills over into the garden.

To the untrained eye, my cluttered cottage garden, which is designed "backward" (made to look best from the house, not from the street), comes across as totally random and disheveled, yet it is celebrated in magazines. It has no lawn at all.

In sharp contrast, one of my neighbors feels compelled to have a strictly maintained landscape, with a neatly mowed and edged lawn and shrubs tightly shorn into identical shapes. And it really looks good, but it demands a lot of maintenance and has little wildlife.

Another neighbor—an educated professional—could not care less about gardening, often going a month or more without even noticing that his grass is spilling out into the street.

The three of us do what we want, and yet we still get along. We respect each others' styles, though privately believing that the others should be more like ourselves. Would things be much better if we gardened alike?

I think not. There will always be folks who prefer curvy lines where their neighbors have straight lines. Folks who like fall colors over showy spring blossoms. Those

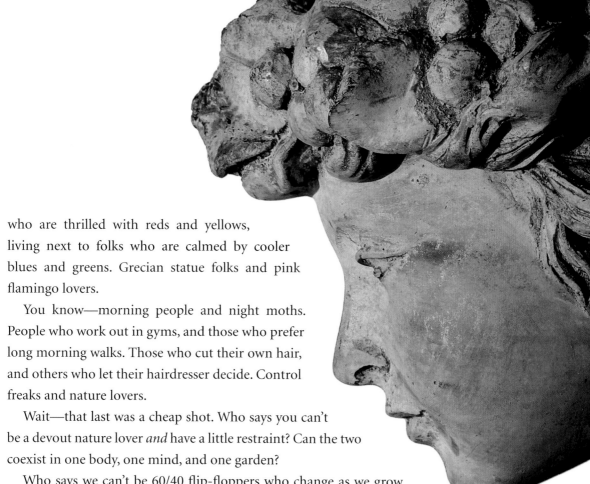

who are thrilled with reds and yellows, living next to folks who are calmed by cooler blues and greens. Grecian statue folks and pink flamingo lovers.

You know—morning people and night moths. People who work out in gyms, and those who prefer long morning walks. Those who cut their own hair, and others who let their hairdresser decide. Control freaks and nature lovers.

Wait—that last was a cheap shot. Who says you can't be a devout nature lover *and* have a little restraint? Can the two coexist in one body, one mind, and one garden?

Who says we can't be 60/40 flip-floppers who change as we grow and mature?

I may end up carving out a small, neat lawn area and scattering a few sheared boxwoods into my naturalistic cottage garden. Who knows? My more orderly neighbor may start to color a little outside the lines by planting a few daffodils in his boxwood border—or even in his lawn.

And we may both learn to appreciate the guy living between us, who has other things on his mind besides gardening.

Living in the Space

Taking the Slow approach in the garden takes a little planning and a lot of tweaking. Whatever kind of landscape you have or want to have—regardless of style, or whether it is designed for relaxation or the pursuit of intense garden hobbies—it should be a place where you feel comfortable, secure, and welcome. The layout of the hard features that make things practical and the plants you choose should work together to lure you outside in all seasons.

The concept of the garden being an extension of your home cannot be overstated. Taking time, or getting professional help, to design the spaces so they will be enticing and practical, and adjusting the smaller details to make them more personal and interesting, will bring more of what you do into focus and make it more enjoyable.

This opens up the garden for better placement and use of plants—the main show, which is what the next chapter is all about.

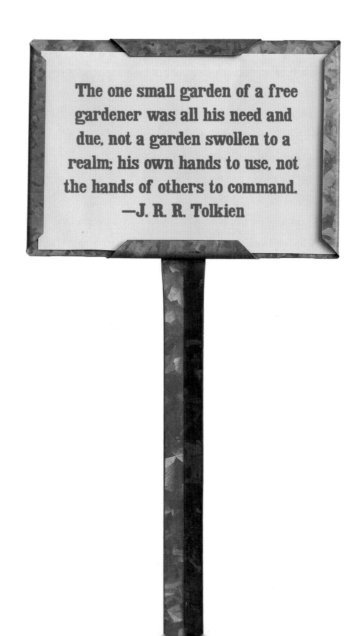

The one small garden of a free gardener was all his need and due, not a garden swollen to a realm; his own hands to use, not the hands of others to command.
—J. R. R. Tolkien

CHAPTER FOUR

Plants— The Real Deal

Slow Gardeners cannot be pegged by the kinds of plants we grow. Yet no matter what our individual garden style or personal preferences—easygoing or up for challenges—we all cherish our plants.

However, it should go without saying that plants are the reason *most* folks take up gardening to begin with. We surround ourselves with plants for their beauty, for the relaxation or therapy they provide, out of curiosity, to attract wildlife, or simply for food. The many different types of plants—and the countless varieties within each type—offer endless opportunities for all these reasons and more.

Unlike the structures, walks, sitting areas, and other "hard" features of the landscape, which form the backbone of everything else, plants— even long-lived trees and shrubs—are considered "soft" features that come and go, change with every season, and require at least some degree of maintenance (even if it's just raking leaves in the fall).

Many plants are so dependable and maintenance-free they can be found in cemeteries—proving what I always like to say, that some plants are so easy even *dead people* can grow them. On the other hand, other plants are so difficult or finicky about their environment that even experts have trouble keeping them alive.

This chapter includes a brief overview of both

common plant types and their uses and a challenge to discover those classic plants that are enjoyed nearly universally by gardeners of all stripes.

"Best" Plant Lists Are Misleading

Some people assume that Slow Gardening means low maintenance, but that is true only for those who choose to go that route. Just as some dog lovers prefer primped poodles while others love any old endearing mutt that wags its tail, some Slow Gardeners cherish zero-input plants while others get their kicks from trying to grow challenging species.

Because of this, no two gardeners will ever agree on a list of "best" or "worst" plants, because of personal experiences and bias. For example, goldenrod (*Solidago canadensis*)—one of North America's most common roadside beauties—is generally considered "weedy" in America (even though it is the official flower of three U.S. states), yet it is one of the most popular summer and fall cut-flower perennials in European gardens. Many new cultivars and hybrids of goldenrod are now available that maximize the ornamental aspects of this plant while curbing the wild species' aggressive tendencies. One gardener can grow tomatoes with no trouble at all, while neighbors struggle with the challenge. My grandmother grew blue-ribbon African violets, but they quickly melt under my hit-or-miss care.

Some plants are so easy to grow that they are considered common or no-class. But instead of holding our noses in the air, we should celebrate them as great "intro" plants for new or beginning gardeners, especially children, who have no expectations, and new home gardeners who are either too busy or horticulturally inexperienced to give them much care. These no-fuss plants are good for starters and often remain popular long after their success has started to wear thin with more advanced gardeners.

I have said many times that it should be considered unethical to give new gardeners hybrid tea roses that are all but guaranteed to do poorly without tender loving care. Start them off instead with proven old shrub roses that all but grow themselves, and let the experience gird the new gardeners for more challenging kinds later on—if they ever graduate upward to the challenges.

Just remember, one gardener's weed is another gardener's wildflower.

Kinds of Plants

Earth laughs in flowers.
—Ralph Waldo Emerson

Experienced gardeners understand that all great gardens include many different kinds of plants.

There are several major categories of plants, based on size or growth habit and use; members of each plant group share broad characteristics, some of which may overlap with those of other kinds of plants. All plants—regardless of whether or not they flower or whether they are evergreen or lose their leaves for part of the year—provide shape, texture, color, seasonal interest, and many other benefits to the garden.

ADVICE TO PLANT-SELECTION NEWBIES

No matter where you learned to garden, if you move even a few miles to a new garden, conditions for growing your favorite plants can change—sometimes dramatically. Forget what you used to know: gardening in a new place can quickly become a whole new game.

To get off on the right foot, start paying attention to what local garden columnists have to say. Swing by the office of the area's university horticulturist, meet the trained volunteers there (called master gardeners in the United States), pick up a few free publications and seasonal newsletters, and look for online calendars of what to do in your new area, and when.

Visit regional botanic gardens, and spend time—preferably over several seasons—exploring your neighborhood to discover the usual palette of plants, noting how well and how big each grows. Take a little time to meet the experienced salespeople at local independent plant nurseries where proven plants are often highlighted during each season.

Most of all, have fun and experiment—and celebrate your failures, because you will learn more from them than from your successes.

A great garden includes many different kinds of plants.

Some are fragrant, produce edible fruit or leaves, attract wildlife, or have important energy-conservation advantages.

In general, plants are either *perennials*, those that can live for many years, even decades, or *annuals*, which either reseed themselves or have to be replanted every year. A few plants fall outside this broad generalization, but most fit neatly somewhere here.

Those long-lived plants with solid trunks and branches—trees, shrubs, and most vines—are generally called "woody" perennials; they form the backbone of most gardens and are selected for their sizes, shapes, colors (both foliage and flowers), and/or fruit.

Woody perennials can be upright or prostrate, climbing or cascading, pointed or roundish, or free-form. Some are evergreen and keep their foliage all year long; others are deciduous and drop their leaves at some point. Designers typically interplant several woodies together to complement one another for year-round landscape effects; some, in fact, actually grow better in the shade of larger ones. Examples of woody perennials include oak trees, roses, and honeysuckle vines.

Herbaceous perennials are those that live for many years but either die down during part of the year (go dormant in hot, cold, or dry weather) or don't really form hard, woody stems. Examples include agaves, daylilies, iris, daffodils, and ornamental grasses. Gardeners often prune or otherwise clean up the aboveground parts of herbaceous perennials when they die back.

In most gardens, annuals—including most vegetables and many herbs—typically live only part of the year before being killed by hot, cold, or dry weather and have to be replanted by seed or by rooted cuttings every year.

Though a few annuals can tolerate extreme cold or extreme heat—at least for a short period—"warm season" annuals, such as tomatoes, zinnias, and basil, which are enjoyed from spring to fall, are usually killed by frost; "cool season" annuals such as cabbage, pansies, and kale can survive just fine in northern climates where summer temperatures stay relatively cool, but most tend to peter out when temperatures rise in the summer and remain high.

In some areas with long growing seasons interrupted by extreme heat or cold, gardeners often replant annuals when the adverse weather passes.

Special Uses for Plants

Though no two gardeners will choose the same kinds of plants for their landscape, plants of all types can be grouped by use for special landscape effects. An effective landscape design will include most or all of the following.

Lawns

Most gardens have a lawn—an expanse of special turfgrass or other extremely low-growing and wear-resistant ground cover—to provide a flat, uncluttered area that opens up and unifies the garden, allows space for butterflies and birds to flutter, and provides people and pets an unimpeded area to walk about and play freely. A neat lawn also serves as a strong unifying element to visually tie everything else together neatly.

In some gardens, the lawn is actually a tiny "throw rug" rather than wall-to-wall carpeting. Some people even grow the grass in large containers, almost like a flat potted plant, where its neat flat greenness makes an interesting foil to other plants—without all the care that's required for a larger lawn.

Because of its need for regular mowing and edging using special equipment, plus the occasional watering, fertilizing, and perhaps weed control, the lawn is typically the garden area with the highest costs in time and expense. Yet it is often also the source of greatest pride, especially in

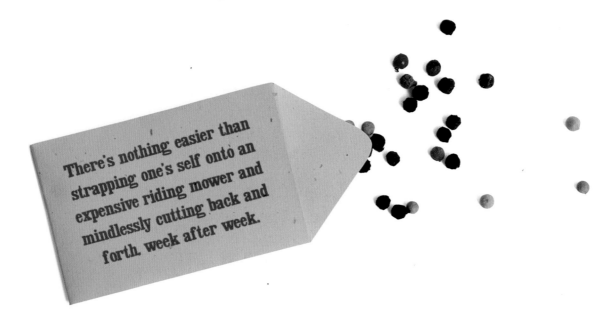

There's nothing easier than strapping one's self onto an expensive riding mower and mindlessly cutting back and forth week after week.

front gardens and other public areas where neighbors often judge a gardener's character simply by the quality of the lawn.

There are quite a few different types of turfgrasses, usually with each having numerous more specialized hybrid varieties. Each type has its own peculiar requirements for mowing height, fertilization, and other kinds of maintenance. Some will tolerate more shade than others, but in general none are adapted for heavy shade, where shade-loving ground covers may be a better choice.

Cool-climate grasses, including ryegrass, fescue, and bluegrass, are "bunching" grasses that grow in little individual tufts. They tolerate cold weather but tend to thin out or die off in heat and humidity. They are typically fertilized in the fall and spring, and they will

The lawn is a dominant feature in most gardens.

"brown out" in dry summer weather but usually green back up after a good rain or with irrigation.

Warm-climate grasses, such as Bermuda grass, centipede, and St. Augustine, are "runner"-type grasses that spread into mats of new plants by rhizomes that root as they grow. Some are available from seed, but all are easily started by the gardener sprigging individual plants or laying mats of sod. They are typically fertilized in late spring and summer and go dormant during cold weather.

The easiest way for an average gardener to gain more weekend time, save money, and help the environment is to get rid of at least part of the lawn.

I'm not an "anti-lawn" curmudgeon—far from it, after years of university training in turf management and decades of consulting with everyone from home lawn owners to golf-course superintendents and other professional athletic-field managers.

It's just that, except for the minority of people who truly get into top-notch lawn care, wall-to-wall turf, though beautiful when done right, is both wasteful—with its greedy demands for time, equipment, water, fertilizer, and weed control—and *boring*. This is why most gardening magazines rarely show landscapes that are more than about one-third to one-half lawn.

Of course, if you are a gardener who simply "mows what grows," who never waters and rarely (if ever) fertilizes, forget all this. It's easy to strap yourself onto an expensive riding mower, cold drink in one hand, and mindlessly cut back and forth, week after week.

A Meadow Lawn Manifesto

Throughout most of the world, the concept of a lawn is simply that of a mat of green vegetation, cut from time to time to keep it reasonably flat. But when Englishman Edwin Budding invented the first lawn mower in the 1850s, things started to change; by the 1950s, with the advent of small, powerful gas engines and chemical herbicides, ordinary home gardeners could afford a neater, lower-maintenance lawn.

Soon, mower manufacturers and fertilizer and chemical-herbicide companies started hammering us with the belief that anyone without a perfectly manicured, weed-free lawn is a lazy failure. An embarrassment to everyone around them.

But given the incredibly polluting exhaust of most gas-guzzling lawn mowers, plus environmental concerns about excessive use of fertilizers, insecticides, herbicides, and fungicides—not to mention the giant slurping sound of irrigation systems sucking our water supplies dry— the "perfect lawn" has now become a symbol of ridiculous excess.

Don't mistake this as a rant; I am not anti-lawn, though I do believe that most people can enjoy a smaller lawn—a throw rug rather than wall-to-wall carpeting—by using ground covers, mulches, trees, and shrubs.

What I am suggesting is a new way to categorize lawns. Currently, they are an either/or scenario—either well-tended or a messy failure. Instead, I believe we need to develop the ethos of having *two different kinds of lawns*, with each being accepted for what it is.

A *turf lawn* would be expected to be regularly mowed and edged, reasonably weed-free, and watered enough to keep it green. Think "golf course putting green."

But there should also be room for a *meadow lawn* style, one that is mowed only when needed, turns brown in drought but greens back up

A seasonal meadow lawn can be attractive as well as low maintenance.

when it rains, and has a light covering of low-growing wildflowers in the winter and spring and a mix of grasses and other relatively low-growing, easy-to-cut plants in the summer.

I mean, isn't this meadow lawn the type most folks already have but won't admit to or accept, for fear of being looked down upon by turf-lawn snobs?

A meadow lawn is like a gardener having informal shrub roses, as compared to row upon row of hybrid tea roses pruned into freakish conformity.

Who would object to this, aside from chemical salespeople and a few obsessive-compulsive neatniks trying to hold everyone else to their own unsustainable, unnecessary standards?

Lawn Care in a Nutshell

All that said, there are people who really get into having a nice lawn and want it to look its best. All you need to do for a decent green covering is to mow what grows, regularly. But to grow a reasonably good-quality lawn, you need to:

- Choose the right type of grass for your part of the world, and select the best variety for your preference.
- Plant well—by seed, sod, plugs, or sprigs—and water enough to get established.
- Mow regularly at the recommended height for your specific kind of grass (perhaps the single most important lawn-care tip). Avoid cutting more than a third to a half of the height of the grass blades at a time. In other words, mow as needed; don't simply wait until the grass gets outrageously long and then crop it short.
- Fertilize lightly with a good organic lawn fertilizer, only during recommended months (check with your university extension office for this information).
- Water slowly and deeply as needed. Keep in mind that too much water, or water applied too often, is usually worse for the lawn than not enough water. Even in dry areas of the country like California and Texas, recommendations are to not water more than once a week—but when you do, water the grass deeply.
- Keep an eye out for problem areas that could indicate insect or disease damage.
- Control weeds as needed—and if desired (there is nothing inherently "wrong" or unethical about having a naturalistic "meadow lawn" full of low-growing wildflowers).
- "Edge" the lawn for a neat appearance (see chapter 3, Edging for a Neater Garden on page 42).
- Sharpen your mower blade at least every couple of months for a clean, crisp cut instead of leaving ragged, dull brown tips.
- Let grass clippings fall back on the lawn. This recycles nutrients and does *not* contribute to "thatch"—really.

Getting Away with a Naturalistic Garden in an Urban Setting

Having trouble cutting loose in your front yard? There's hope, in precedent-setting gardens that have successfully broken the mold most landscapes have been stuck in since the 1930s.

Having little or no lawn is no longer all that unconventional, especially in older neighborhoods where deepening shade has petered out most of the grass, and folks have the wherewithal and confidence to try something different. My neighborhood is packed with gardens that have ground covers, shrubs, and even swaths of wildflowers, including in front of expensive homes on well-heeled streets.

Too bad this isn't the case in much of suburbia, home of look-alike "Stepford" gardens where folks are pressured to fit in with interchangeable same old, same old; however, as more people get comfortable seeing small flowering shrubs, hardy perennials, and ornamental grasses, things are shifting toward more color and texture—even in front yards.

Want to see some good examples? Cruise around older, upscale neighborhoods, nicely landscaped restaurants, and even fast-food restaurants and service stations, where if you pay attention you will see less grass, which is very expensive to mow, edge, water, and spray for weeds, and more groups of hardy plants with year-round appeal, plus lots of mulch and ground covers.

Even a small amount of meadow lawn can be attractive while reducing maintenance needs of wall-to-wall turfgrass.

I don't really care whether this is becoming a lasting trend because of changing aesthetics or because it is laborsaving and cost-effective; it's all good.

However, getting started can be daunting. Believe me, there is nothing like the ire of a neatnik neighbor—or an unenlightened, overzealous city inspector—to bring you down. Happens all the time.

But there are successful precedents, and now plenty of what lawyers call "case law" to help those of you who want to be free from the ennui of landscape conformity.

Here are a few strategies that can help you get away with having a naturalistic garden in an urban setting:

- Check local ordinances or neighborhood restrictions, but don't be intimidated by definitions of a "weed." (Remember, there is little difference botanically or horticulturally between a bed full of roses and daylilies and a neatly tended wildflower garden.)
- Have a plan. Don't just let stuff grow up. Show and discuss the plan with neighbors and city inspectors.

THE NO-DIG APPROACH TO NEW BEDS

Sometimes it just seems like too hard a chore to dig up an area of thick lawn to start a new flower bed. There is a way to do this without digging at all.

This "no-dig" bed preparation, long advocated by "permaculture" advocates, is simple. Cover the area with layers of flattened cardboard, then cover that with fallen tree leaves several inches thick. It will instantly look neat while smothering grass and weeds, and within weeks—certainly the next spring—the soil underneath will be soft, rich, teeming with earthworms, and ready to plant into.

When you're ready to plant, set out plants six to twelve inches apart, fill in with mulch, and water and weed as needed, and before long you'll have made a nice-looking transition from lawn to flower beds.

- Get assistance from a licensed land-scape designer, area native-plant enthusiasts, wildlife proponents, or other authorities.
- Plant trees and shrubs in natu-ralistic groupings, with lots of mulch to keep weeds down.
- Include an attractive "hard" feature (sculpture, bird bath, section of fence, large rock, wagon wheel, etc.) as a year-round focal point.
- Grow vines on approved or nice-looking structures.
- Leave a neat "mowing strip" between your landscape and public areas or neigh-bors' yards.
- Include showy, familiar nonnative plants that give a feeling of comfort to other viewers (daylilies, irises, daffodils, roses, etc.).

An official sign from the National Wildlife Federation lends credibility to a naturalistic garden.

- Provide water and nesting areas for wildlife. Have the garden certified as a "Backyard Wildlife Habitat" (contact the National Wildlife Federation for guidelines and a placard that lets neighbors know you are doing all this on purpose).
- Maintain the area as neatly as you can—remember, it's naturalistic, not wild.
- Respond quickly and firmly, but politely, to complaints.
- Invite friends and neighbors over from time to time to help them feel comfortable.

Ground Covers

Various plants that grow relatively flat or low are often massed together as ground covers in areas that are shady, steeply sloped, or otherwise

Ground covers are great alternatives for places where a lawn would be difficult or impractical.

unsuitable for lawns. Generally evergreen, most ground covers spread well, help prevent erosion, and provide interesting, often colorful alternatives to turfgrasses or mulch.

I know some folks love mowing the lawn—believe me, I get e-mails every time I get on a rant about wall-to-wall grass or other "same old, same old" landscape clichés. And some folks need a big lawn area for the kids to play on.

But come on—surely even the most staid landscape can use a little diversity! Besides, in places where land and/or water is precious, people tend to use the lawn as a green "throw rug" that unifies the garden, rather than dominating it.

Anyway, with a nod to folks who really do love their lawns, many others have areas that are too big to fertilize, water, and mow properly, that are too steep or dangerous to mow, or that are too shady for grass.

This is where mulches, paving, decks, walks, flowerbeds, and ground covers come in. They not only take up space, but also create interest and lower the maintenance needs of the lawn. And mulches and ground covers don't have to be extensive to make a lawn more interesting and easier to maintain.

Most ground covers take two or three years to fill in (first year they sleep, second year they creep, third year they leap). But once done, they're done for good. Check with local experts for recommendations on suitable groundcovers that are not too invasive for your area.

Here is a simple design trick: instead of carving flower, shrub, and ground cover areas out of the lawn, *make the lawn the shape*. Use your mower to determine the right curves, and let whatever can't be mowed easily become the "other plants" areas. It will look more professional and be a lot easier to maintain.

Potted Plants

Slow Gardeners usually include potted plants—both indoors and out— to expand the selection of plants we can grow through the seasons. Specialty potting soils and our ability to move pots in and out of doors help us grow a wide variety of unusual plants, and in settings where space or natural soils are limited.

Vegetables and herbs, and even fruit plants, can be grown in pots on sunny porches, and container gardens can be planted and replanted easily without a lot of tools or labor.

Most of us learned at an early age how to grow simple plants in pots, from the first time a school teacher showed us how to put a bean seed in a milk carton. We learned to give it a little sunshine, some water when it got dry, and a little "plant food" to help it grow.

Then it usually died, which set us up for expecting failure with adult plants, from poinsettias and African violets given to us as gifts, to floppy paper-white narcissus, to all those macramé hanger plants that were such a craze in the 1960s and '70s. And when we or a family member came home from the hospital with one of those mixed pots of baby tropical plants—usually a heart-

Tropical plants can be grown well outside their natural range in containers.

leaf philodendron, a small palm, a mother-in-law's tongue, and a prayer plant—the prayer plant quickly gave up the ghost.

Then, when that mother-in-law's tongue (known botanically as *Sansevieria*) survived, and the heart-leaf philodendron vine began spreading all around the window, we learned that there are a good many plants that actually thrive in the low-light, low-humidity, cool-temperature spaceship environments we call home.

Other Ways to Use Plants

Often, accent plants with a unique shape (either natural or pruned) or color are used to create a strong visual focal point to draw interest to a particular spot in the garden. These strikingly attractive plants can also be used as a diversion to keep people from noticing something less

THE HELL STRIP

Gardeners get irked when plants refuse to step up and overcome challenging situations. But plants themselves face more than frustration when forced into daunting settings: they can suffer or even die.

Ghastly sites for both plants and gardeners include dense shade with tree root competition, heavy clay or exposed subsoil, dry slopes, and low areas that are boggy all winter long but dry into cracked dust in the summer. Oh, and then there's the low humidity and light that's found in offices, or atop the home television.

But the only trouble spot referred to by horticulturists as the "hell strip" is that little grassy strip between the street and the sidewalk. More than a challenge for designers, it's sheer misery for plants: hard-packed dirt, no room for roots, and intense reflected heat retained by pavement all night, and often the only moisture is from rain or roaming dogs.

Yet that little sliver is useful. Beyond increasing pedestrian safety, it's ideal for keeping fire hydrants, street signs, mailboxes, telephone poles, and garbage cans out of the way of walkers. It's also a convenient place to pile leaves (or snow) seasonally. And it reduces the amount of muddy "road splash" flung onto people by cars after a rain.

Planting living stuff in these little strips of dirt is encouraged by a lot of cities, both to serve as a buffer between people and traffic and to beautify and "soften" the streetscape; it also discourages parking on a bare area, which is illegal in some places.

The first thing most folks plant is grass, which quickly devolves into weeds in constant need of mowing and edging. Mulches are okay there, as are bricks or other pavers, but most folks want real plants—few of which really want to be there.

Small shrubs, evergreen ground covers, perennials, and bulbs generally need to stand under about three feet in height and must tolerate being stumbled over to survive here. Dwarf hollies and spreading junipers, along with daffodils, artemisia, small daylilies (like 'Stella D'Oro' and other varieties), and other drought- and heat-tolerant plants tolerate these conditions.

University extension service offices have lists available of recommended "street trees" that don't disrupt pavement and are easy to keep pruned (because joggers, the elderly, and the sight-impaired take precedence over low limbs in this public planting zone). It's always important to look up before planting trees, as overhead utility lines are a tree's worst nightmare.

Only a few plants are well adapted to harsh, hot, dry growing conditions.

attractive nearby. Special effects can be created by judiciously repeating these accents throughout even a very small garden.

Hedges are simply "living walls" made of similar or mixed shrubs or trees that are planted close together and usually pruned to remain upright and narrow. When made of mixed plants, hedges can become important wildlife habitats.

Vines are the climbers of the garden, and they can be used to tone down tall structures, help shade sunny walls, and provide other "vertical" enhancements. Whether evergreen or deciduous, whether grown for foliage, flowers, or fruit (tomato plants, after all, are vines), they require supports to grow on. Some twine themselves or attach to supports with rootlike tendrils; others have to be tied as they grow.

Whether planted up against something else (wall, trees, hedge, patio) or out in the lawn, flower beds are man-made mixed-plant "verges" that create opportunities for a wide variety of fairly small plants—including wildflowers and small flowering shrubs—to mix and mingle for strong visual effects. Borders are generally long flower beds set against a wall or hedge.

Though most gardeners think of vegetables and herbs as special plant groups, the various plants—as well as cut flowers—can easily be mixed into flower beds and borders. However, since they usually require regular, intensive planting, tending, and harvesting, it is often easier to manage them when they're grouped into special plots, often in long, easy-to-work rows, raised beds, or containers.

Other special-use plants include orchards and vineyards for fruit growing; collections for plant-society members, serious hobbyists, and hybridizers who love certain plants over most others; plants to attract wildlife; plants to collect and reduce water runoff in rain gardens; and aquatic plants in water ponds.

Vegetables as Ornamental Plants

Why don't more people grow stuff to actually *eat*? Could be because we think that growing vegetables and herbs is not only difficult but also, well, vaguely related to agriculture. Which it most certainly is not.

True, it has been for the past handful of generations. But down through the centuries most folks simply grew food and flavorings without being anywhere near a farm. They treated these edible plants simply

Hedges—sheared or naturalistic—create strong barriers and enclosures.

as plants—no different from marigolds or daylilies—to be set out when the weather was right and taken care of before and during harvests.

I don't have a single "row" of plants of any kind anywhere in my garden, just lots of flower beds and containers of all sizes and descriptions planted a little at a time—no sweat or heavy equipment involved. But right now, mixed in with dozens of different "ornamental" plants, I also have cabbage, lettuce, onions, parsley, rosemary, chives, garlic chives, potatoes, kale, mustard, garlic, and oregano—all perfectly at home in the mild winters in my state.

I have a particular affinity for heirloom vegetables, many of which are not widely available in grocery stores. Odd-colored tomatoes with extraordinary flavor, exotic lettuces, 'Moon and Stars' watermelon (with its large yellow spot and extra-sweet flesh), tasty ancient hot peppers, elephant garlic (which is technically a type of belowground leek), heat-loving Malabar spinach, and beans with beautiful purple or red flowers as well as crunchy pods: these and more are both pretty and delicious, and because they are "open-pollinated" (non-hybrid varieties) I can save seed for next year or to share or swap with other gardeners.

I plant tomatoes, basil, and six different kinds of peppers, along with sweet potatoes, eggplant (including a really ornamental white kind), and even three kinds of okra. Most are varieties that look as good as they taste—a key to enjoying these culinary plants in what would otherwise be considered a "flower" garden. I've even grown variegated sweet corn like a regular ornamental grass—right in the front yard!

The secret? Instead of treating these edible and herbal plants like row crops, I simply interplant them in regular garden spots. I stick them right in with my irises, daylilies, periwinkle, salvia, pansies, and other flowers.

Vegetable and herb gardens can be attractive as well as productive.

There are several advantages of this mixed-garden approach (which the French call *potager* gardening): interesting, easy, year-round beauty; steady production without all the hassles of tilling and preparing for one-shot row crops; fewer pests because the plants are mixed in with "non-target" plants; and, if something gets harvested or dies, it's camouflaged with other flowers so nobody can tell! All I have to do is pull the plants up and replant in the same hole or container!

This approach isn't farming, it's *gardening*!

Vertical Gardening

What can you do on a budget for a fast impact in the garden? *Look up!*

Is your eye naturally drawn to the furthest point on your property? If not, then that's naturally the best place to set a bold object. With or without vines growing over it, anything vertical gives instant eye-catching gratification and can be quite inexpensive.

It doesn't take much to create a strong effect: a large structure such as an arbor or trellis will up the visual ante, but it may not be necessary.

A recently revived trend toward growing plants on rooftops and walls—like what was done for centuries by people who lived in sod houses or had root cellars—is merely a variation on container gardening, done atop sealed roofs and walls; it requires special attention to construction, soils, watering, and plant selection.

But to have a simple arbor or post effect, start with the idea of a single post, either painted to match the trim of your house for that all-important "repetition" effect or in a bold, contrasting color that creates a strong focal point. A square or round post topped with a flat piece of flagstone and a bold piece of pottery may be all you need to draw texture and attention to an otherwise dull, two-dimensional planting.

The bolder the materials, the stronger the effect: 4×4 posts may be your first choice for arbor material, but 4×6—or better yet, 6×6—posts look more solid and professional, less like a weekend project. You'll get more "oomph" for just a little more money.

In fact, for a really solid effect in my own little garden I use tall, six-inch-wide iron I beams sunk three feet deep in the ground and anchored in concrete. The rusted posts are so bold that they tone down my junkiest plantings and lend an air of strength to the whole scene.

Walls can be turned into living vertical gardens.

Even wooden posts need to be sunk at least eighteen inches in the ground, with a sack of ready-mix concrete around each one—especially if they are to support much weight like an arbor or swing. And the taller the better—a vine arbor needs to be at least eight feet high for people to walk under it after the vines mature. Higher is better.

If you want to train a vine or two to grow up your posts (again, not necessary), there are lots of possibilities. But whether you plant on it or not, putting something vertical in the back corner of your yard, or out a few feet from your front porch, quickly makes a big difference in how your garden appears.

Herbs

Herbs and vegetables aren't special classes of plants—they are just individual plants with various attributes or uses other than good looks. You may already grow some herbs without realizing it: How many of us grow iris but have never used its dried root as a powdered herbal fixative? How many people use the foliage of yarrow to wrap cuts and scrapes? Few folks wash their hair with soapwort or clean their teeth with horsetail, even though for centuries that's what they were used for. Nowadays we grow them as regular landscape plants, not herbs.

For that matter, many perfectly edible flowers, including violas, daylilies, redbud, and roses, are grown because they're pretty, not because you can eat them.

Hmmm. I wonder . . . if a four-leaf clover really can bring good luck, does that make it a herb?

To me, a herb isn't a herb unless you use it as such, any more than a bicycle is transportation if you don't actually ride it.

The Companion-Plant Coalition

It seems like every plant on earth has its cheerleaders who think their favorite plant and its cousins are superior to all the rest. Everything else in Eden is relegated to being mere "companion plants," playing bit parts as supporters to the main actor. You know these types of gardeners, who are not satisfied unless their rows upon rows of cherished greenery are punctuated with neat labels proclaiming this or that cultivar of the newest, latest, or greatest.

While I love roses—especially the disease-resistant ever-blooming shrub types that fit in anywhere with little fuss—I am aware that most people first try the fussier hybrid teas that seem to melt with black spot all over the world. When folks plant these, and the plants fail, the gardeners often feel to blame and give up on roses altogether.

Don't get me wrong . . . I have been a member and even past president of several plant societies; I have extensive collections of several types of plants (over seventy different daffodils alone), and I actually do enjoy growing improved varieties of different plants. I have hybrid roses, daylilies, irises— even specially developed cultivars of native plants never found in the wild.

When it comes to daylilies, I really admire the long-blooming miniatures like 'Stella d'Oro', which is universally grown but largely eschewed by daylily society members as cliché. (There are no cliché plants, only cliché gardeners.) Still, my all-time favorite daylily is the old double orange 'Kwanso', grown for eons as a nutritious food (more vitamins than broccoli!) and actually mass-planted outside the royal gardens at Kew in London. Though nearly impossible to find in a daylily-society display, it grows for me, you, anybody, anywhere, with absolutely no demands. None.

Still, there are those folks who look beyond mere beauty and fragrance toward the challenges of newer and more interesting varieties, who love to get together and cheer one another on, forming clubs and societies centered around one type of plant, with standards and guidelines . . . and a dab of disdain, if not downright snobbery, toward all others who don't garden as intensively or competitively.

In my egalitarian garden, where every plant has the right to its pursuit of sunlight and admiration, I try to grow 'em all. Camellias, irises, daylilies, roses, herbs, native plants, daffodils, hellebores, cacti and succulents, hibiscus, philodendrons, heirloom tomatoes and peppers, palms, and bromeliads. I grow them as individuals—just good plants, not competitors.

That's enough to have a cherished plant-society representative in bloom every week of the year. A plant-society garden, so to speak.

Hmmm. If there were a Compost Club, and maybe a Weed Lovers' Alliance, I could be a member of those, too.

I guess what I'd like to see would be a Garden Variety Gardener's Guild, in which only folks who love all plants equally could belong. Better yet, we could call it the Companion-Plant Coalition!

Herbs don't have to be grown just in herb gardens.

By the way, I pronounce the *h* in *herb*, like my English ancestors—not like the French who drop the letter. Ee-ther or I-ther way is fine (the only way to be incorrect is by correcting someone else).

After working with herb and vegetable growers, both amateur home gardeners and professionals (even in botanic gardens), for many years, and growing too many herbs to count in my own gardens, I've settled down to a few that are personally satisfying and easy to grow, and that I actually use.

My toughest garden herbs, which take both summer and winter conditions in the Deep South, include rosemary (which makes a sizeable bush), bay laurel, oregano, chives, garlic chives, mints, garlic (which I plant in the fall, along with cold-hardy parsley), thyme, and Mexican tarragon or Mexican mint marigold. Every summer I also plant several kinds of basil.

There are other easy and useful herbs, of course, but these are the ones that are most useful to me. All grow best in well-drained flower beds or containers, with at least six to seven hours of direct sunlight, a tiny amount of fertilizer, and only occasional soakings. When I set out transplants, I always loosen their roots and potting soil and mulch after planting.

The main point is, you don't have to be a farmer, or even have a dedicated vegetable or herb garden, to enjoy wonderful and edible plants as regular flowers.

> A herb isn't a herb unless you use it as such, any more than a bicycle is transportation if you don't actually ride it.

Wildflowers Come to Town

> *In the hope of reaching the moon men fail*
> *to see the flowers that blossom at their feet.*
> —Albert Schweitzer

While walking around the neighborhood the other day, I was surprised at how many native plants are being used like "normal" plants in flower beds.

But then I should not have been, since so many are just plain pretty and easy to grow—on top of being naturally adapted to our soils and weather.

Plants for People Who Like Tending Plants

There are certain people who love tending plants. And there are certain plants that require coddling. Sometimes it's good to get the two groups together.

For decades now I have championed hardy, tough-as-nails trees, shrubs, perennials, annuals, and even potted houseplants that all but take care of themselves—plants that are not taskmasters and therefore free us up to enjoy our gardens more.

But, in the spirit of "different strokes for different folks," I acknowledge those persons who genuinely revel in attention to detail and pride in workmanship, who thrill in discovering new minutiae in the garden.

These are the folks who count rose petals, or who edge their lawns every week. Gardeners afflicted with a compulsion to categorize—like stamp collectors—which causes them to seek out and display as many different varieties of, say, iris, daffodil, or Japanese maple as possible.

There's nothing wrong with this behavior, of course. At least I hope not, because I'm troubled myself; I have "only" around seventy different daffodils, forty-plus roses, and fourteen sansevierias. And I collect manure from famous thoroughbred horses to enrich my *primo* compost. Really.

Anyway, let's admit it: Anyone can strap themselves onto a riding mower with a beer in one hand and cut a "mow what grows" lawn. But it takes dedication to have a uniformly manicured, weed-free lawn.

And while hundreds of landscape plants (especially natives) can survive on very little care, I freely acknowledge that most will grow and perform better when tended occasionally with watering, fertilizing, pruning, and the like.

Some plants, however, all but demand high levels of maintenance, rewarding gardeners who lavish great care and grooming on them; most of these will quickly peter out and die if given only spotty attention.

And there are people who cherish the challenge. Therefore, I propose a list of exceptionally demanding plants that *require* a modicum of upkeep: regular watering, special temperatures, deft pruning, constant feeding with specialty fertilizers, vigilant pest/disease control, or whatever. These are Plants for People Who Need the Therapy.

My starter contenders would include hybrid tea roses, serious lawns, topiary shrubs and bonsai plants, African violets, orchids, hanging baskets, peaches, and prize-winning vegetables.

I'd also consider including plants with confusing (to most garden-variety gardeners) pruning instructions. Put 'em on at least an honorable-mention list. Hydrangeas, clematis, and figs fit in here, at least according to all the calls I get about them.

I'm only partly kidding here, folks. The point is that Slow Gardening, being inclusive, has room even for folks who take pride in fulfilling their need to overcome challenges.

Hobby plants such as bonsai are difficult but fascinating.

It's not just the trees and shrubs, either, though there are lots of oaks, magnolias, birches, cedars, cypress, buckeyes, and native yaupon hollies, plus oak-leaf hydrangeas, sweet shrub, wax myrtle, cherry laurel, blueberries, flowering prickly pear cactus, and yucca. All native.

These are what I call "backbone" plants of the garden, giving shape and texture while framing the house. Most are well adapted for both sun and shade and the natural rainfall and drought cycles.

I'm not a hard-core native plants advocate, though my garden certainly has more than its share. But they do lend an exciting sense of place that centers me and makes me feel at home in my native land.

When I started gardening on my postage-stamp lot in an older, artsy part of town, I killed off the existing lawn and replaced it with large boulders, natural mulch, and wildflowers. On purpose.

I grow many of the most beautiful plants on Earth, which can be found right around me along country roads and riverbanks, in fields and woods. These natives—including trees, shrubs, vines, perennials, annuals, and even bulbs and grasses—are naturally well suited for my climate, my soils, and my laziness; after all, they have been growing for thousands of years without artificial life support, long before I started taking an interest in their beauty.

Not only are many of them useful as landscape plants, but most are also attractive to the native wildlife, including birds, bees, hummingbirds, butterflies, spiders, wasps, and everything else that flits or wanders by.

Native plants are a win/win/win situation for all concerned.

But the natives are getting restless. First the dwarf, clump-forming yucca began crowding the boulders. Then my cherished goldenrod, the pride of many a European perennial border, started coloring outside the lines, and the liatris,

Wildflowers can be tamed for urban use through simple landscape tricks such as adding a fence or other naturalistic object and including some familiar garden plants.

So fair, so sweet, withal so sensitive,
Would that the little flowers were
born to live,
Conscious of half the pleasure which
they give …

—William Wordsworth

asters, showy evening primrose, spiderwort, and narrow-leaf sunflowers followed suit.

Blackberry vines, which I now tolerate for their showy spring flowers and summer fruit, arrived as seed in wild bird droppings but have begun vying for more than their allotted space. Broom sedge and river oats, two of my favorite native grasses for winter texture, began cropping up along the edges of my berm and in cracks of the driveway.

I managed to get a grip on the poison ivy that appeared one spring, but the Virginia creeper, Carolina jessamine ("yellow jasmine"), and cross vine are tangling with my brilliant fall-colored sumac—beautifully, but far from neatly.

And to top it off, I've had to spend time prying tree seedlings from it all: post oaks from one neighbor, willow oaks from across the street, cherry laurel and yaupon hollies from the birds, and hackberries and wild cherries from who knows where.

These days we don't have to be nuts to grow and enjoy beautiful native wildflowers in modern gardens. It's only natural. But on occasion we may need to curb their enthusiasm and check their overexuberant growth.

Invasive Exotics: Pandora's Box

Few gardens outlive their gardener, but many plants outlive the garden.
—Roger Swain

Be careful of any plant that someone wants to give you a LOT of.

In North America, the generally accepted definition of a "native" plant is any plant that was found on the continent before the late 1400s, when Europeans began introducing plants from afar. It's very general, because a lot of nonnative plants were blown by seed or carried by birds to the continent, and even some Native Americans were swapping seeds from Central and South America long before Christopher Columbus first set sail.

But back in 1871, a group of guys got together in New York City to form the American Acclimatization Society, the purpose of which was to deliberately introduce new species of birds, animals, and plants to America.

Their intentions—to bring in birds that could eat the bugs and other pests on area grains—were good at the time, but they had no idea how quickly some would multiply and spread, and then displace native creatures. This is how many of our favorite plants were introduced, ranging from azaleas to zinnias. Most are well behaved, but some turned into thugs, or "weeds." Fortunately, most exuberant plants can be contained with a little judicious pulling; only a few get out of economical control.

For example, in the 1880s, kudzu was introduced through the Pennsylvania Horticulture Society's flower show as a fantastic climbing vine. But then our government paid people to plant the fast-growing vine across the Southeast for erosion control. Just a few decades later, it has caused incredible losses to Southeastern forests, with no control in sight.

And purple loosestrife, introduced as an ornamental plant from Europe, has choked out thousands of acres of natural wetlands in colder climates.

Those introduced plants that easily escape cultivation or otherwise begin to "take over" nearby areas—natural areas, recreational areas, or commercial agriculture or fishing grounds—are considered "invasive" exotics, and they are often put on restricted or even banned plant lists compiled by regional environmental groups or government agencies.

Every region has introduced plants, like this kudzu vine, that have escaped the garden to become serious threats to the countryside.

Typically, invasive plants grow rapidly, spread quickly and easily by seed or vegetatively (runners), are expensive or difficult to remove or control, and outcompete and take over native species; they often disrupt agriculture and ruin recreational sites, destroy native wildlife habitats, and change entire ecosystems.

Land managers, scientists, foresters, farmers, ecologists, conservationists, outdoor sportsmen, and educators are joining together to identify and combat these aliens. And government publications have strong language for those people who love all plants regardless of country of origin: *never buy those plants that you suspect are nonnative.*

However, to those who would insist—even under penalty of law—that we never grow certain plants, consider this thought: "When ivy is outlawed, only outlaws will grow ivy."

I'm not saying we shouldn't be concerned about serious weeds, and I agree that we should take action. You can start by going online to find a list of the worst "invasive exotics" offenders.

But the bottom line is that responsible gardeners will avoid growing plants that pose serious threats should they escape the garden—even unintentionally by seed spread by the wind or birds.

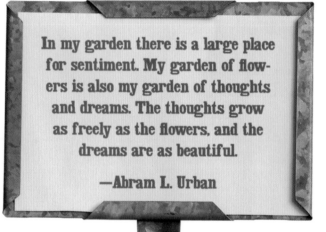

In my garden there is a large place for sentiment. My garden of flowers is also my garden of thoughts and dreams. The thoughts grow as freely as the flowers, and the dreams are as beautiful.

—Abram L. Urban

Pass-Along Plants: Comfort Food for the Gardener's Soul

Folks who don't have daylilies, hostas, or irises must not have many gardening friends. Gardeners share, *period*. As much as we love getting new plants, we are obligated to pass some along to others. It's more than just goodwill or a karma thing—it's also an outlet for our excess, and it helps us hone our propagation skills.

Plus, it spreads around and preserves a little of the diversity found in backyard gardens, as opposed to the bland, relative paucity that comes from most landscapers and gardeners using the same mass-produced *plants du jour*. This can help reduce the oh-so-familiar problems that come from too many people growing a lot of the same things over and over, risking an American elm disease or potato blight crash.

What's interesting—and comforting—to know is that even though a good many gardeners are "nonjoiners" who don't belong to garden clubs or plant societies, aren't university-trained master gardeners, and may not work well with or even like other people all that much, we still find ways to share plants and gardening tips with one another.

In fact, it should be noted that swapping plants is perhaps the only thing we *truly* share—including language, music, clothing styles, food, and the like—that so completely crosses cultural, racial, religious, gender, or any other lines that keep people apart.

A quick survey of neighborhood gardens in any part of the country will uncover many dozens of these universally grown plants.

Compared with the hundreds of possibilities of great, easily grown

GARDENERS LOVE TO CHAT

Working on a National Endowment for the Arts grant, I spent part of one summer working a small Southern town from one end to the other, exploring how people of diverse ethnic, racial, economic, and educational backgrounds share garden plants, lore, and techniques. A reporter for a New York-based newspaper followed me around for a week and marveled at how easy it can be to knock boldly on doors of strangers and start conversations about their gardens.

"You gotta believe," I explained, "that the gardener in each of us *wants* to come out. The trick is in making that good spirit feel safe."

I always carry in hand a flower or branch of some plant that is common to the neighborhood and start with, "Excuse me, but I see this growing all over the place and wonder if you can tell me what you call it." This leads naturally to how or from where the plant came to the gardener being interviewed, and before long a relaxed conversation will usually ensue.

You just have to believe in—and lean on—a gardener's innate curiosity and helpfulness.

ON FINDING NEW PLANTS

How do you find new plants? Whether you like trees, shrubs, or vines; herbaceous perennials; bulbs, grasses, or tender annuals; vegetables or herbs; or potted tropical plants, there is only so much room or time to plant and care for new stuff. So how do you decide what to plant?

I have my own system for evaluating new garden plants, based on trial and error from half a century of being exposed, via a hard-gardening extended family, to the oldest and toughest "tried and true" pass-along plants from my family's gardens and country and "po' folk" gardens. Add to that my close observations of native plants that look great in the landscape (both in the United States and abroad), three decades of commercial nursery and garden-center work and consultations, all my university horticulture training, and having visited thousands—and lectured in hundreds—of gardens, both great and small, around the world.

Truth is, I'm always attracted to plants, old or new, mainly by gut feelings—how they make me smile, whether or not my brain tells me they are "good" for me or my garden.

But when one catches my eye, either in a local garden or garden center or in a faraway place, I go through the same process: Do I think it will grow in my climate and soil? Do I have to dig a special hole, or will it grow in just plain dirt? Will I have to do a lot of watering to keep it alive? Will it "come back" on its own, or do I like it enough to replant it every year?

Then I decide if I have room for it: Where will it fit, what will it look good beside, how big will it get—both tall and wide? Will it take over and become a problem to keep in bounds, or is it so pretty it doesn't really matter?

Will it have a lot of pest problems? This is one area where the answer really does matter, because I do not want to spend time and money on pesticides when there are so many great plants that are relatively problem-free. I may be foolish for plants, but I'm not a fool.

Bottom line is, if I see it and want it badly enough, I'll give it a try. If it works, I'll urge others to try it; if it doesn't, well, there's my compost pile, and something down the road that'll fit in that hole.

plants for a given area, many local garden centers carry a fairly limited selection of "eye candy" plants based on how well they sell on curb appeal alone. Too often, these plants are not well adapted to "garden variety" garden conditions and end up being short-lived. Most depend on a lot of soil preparation, fertilizing, careful watering, and pest control, and still they die—often taking with them the gardener's hopes and confidence.

Yet for thousands of years before garden centers, countless individual gardeners have been saving, planting, and sharing heirloom vegetables, herbs, flowers, fruits, and other valued landscape plants, often passed down for generations within a single family or community.

Defying the "copycat" effect, in which people grow those currently popular "fast food" plants, these hearty plants perform and are enjoyed by gardeners *in spite of* their lack of commercial appeal. In fact, many of these old "comfort food" plants that have come and gone in popular favor— including those once valued as medicinal herbs—are now surging in popularity because of their durability as well as their often subtle beauty and long-ago practical uses.

Many plants, like this *Iris albicans*, were introduced for one reason but ended up being widely used for their toughness and simple beauty.

Few gardeners use the rhizomes of the ancient white iris (*Iris albicans*) as a herbal fixative or wash their hair with suds made from soapwort (*Saponaria officinalis*), yet these plants remain as mainstays of hardy perennial borders and rock gardens.

Often these plants have unique traits that are hard to find in plants on the mass market. Sometimes their fruits, though misshapen and off-color, have superior flavor; have you ever marveled at how much better certain old varieties of tomatoes grown at home or found at local farmers' markets seem to taste, compared with those grown and shipped from afar that are found, out of season, in supermarkets? And who hasn't seen an old rose blooming in gardens all over the countryside—grown by many different gardeners because it is simply pretty—that is not available for sale at garden centers?

There is a name for these dependable performers that are not generally sold anywhere yet are grown by nearly everyone: pass-along plants.

Pass-along plants usually have four important characteristics: value, adaptation to a wide variety of soils and settings, freedom from major pests, and ease of propagation.

Value

Value simply means the plant is worth something to someone. It could have a more intense flavor or fragrance or be easy to harvest or prepare for cooking (peas that are easy to shell, for instance); it could be a superior cut flower, or perhaps it blooms in the evening when folks are most likely to be around to admire it. It could be a great butterfly or humming-bird attractor, or a beautiful roadside or woodland native plant worth being cultivated.

Some people keep a plant around just for its story. Perhaps it is an heirloom passed down by family members, rescued from an old homeplace, or brought home from vacation. Maybe it's just a cutting of something that was grown by someone famous.

The more values a plant has, the more people will choose to grow it.

The main thing is, the more values a plant has, the more different kinds of people will want to grow it.

Adaptation

Adaptation to a wide variety of soils, climates, and other growing conditions ensures that more people with fewer gardening skills can enjoy growing a particular plant. Many old pass-along plants have proven themselves to be dependable without a lot of horticultural life support.

If a plant requires a lot of soil preparation, watering, fertilizing, pruning, deadheading, training, covering during frosts, or other extraordinary gardening effort, only a few dedicated dilettantes will grow it for long.

I have long forgotten whose idea it was, but many years ago I adopted a simple test for plant hardiness: set it in its pot on the driveway out back for two summers and one winter, and if it's still alive after that time, it goes to the front of the queue for planting in the ground somewhere.

FLOWER SHOWS FOR IDEAS

I have trouble telling a "bad good" idea from a "good bad" idea. But as I travel about I often see them both, and everything in between—especially when I visit flower shows where top designers put everything (including the kitchen sink) into their creative showcases.

There are flower and plant society displays of course, where countless new plant introductions can be compared with standard varieties. Usually the proud growers are standing nearby, all but begging for frank conversations about their plants.

But I go straight to the showcase gardens to note what is hot in the coolest new plants and latest ideas in garden design. Trying to stay on top of trends, I note those plants I think would grow well for folks in my part of the world and encourage growers to provide a few for garden centers to try on their customers.

But in these display gardens, some of which are miniatures with ideas very well suited for my own little garden, I am also exposed to a lot of combinations and concepts that would never occur to me on my own. Some are serious, almost staid; others are whimsical, even humorous. All are thought-provoking.

Lately it seems as if all the flower shows feature "green" ecological themes involving recycling, reducing water use, and other sustainable gardening techniques—even small-scale food production, usually in small raised beds or containers.

Every single display garden—some of which are larger than my own front yard and cost tens of thousands of dollars to install for just the few days of the show—includes common elements that designers consider

de rigueur for good gardening: small, well-defined lawn areas, overstuffed containers, vines and other vertical features, funky tool and potting sheds, and so on.

And water. They nearly all have some source of visible water—a hallmark of a good garden (and a requirement for attracting wildlife). Because I enjoy several water features in my own little cottage garden, I am always looking for fun new ideas. I see recycled containers of every description turned into reflective pools or cascading water fountains, but my favorites are the capricious ones: water spurting from sculptures, spilling from musical instruments, or gushing out of wine bottles.

Are those good ideas, or bad? I don't know. But flower shows both large and small are crucial for discovering new plant and design ideas.

Flower shows are great places to see new or interesting varieties of different kinds of plants—even vegetables.

PLANTS DEAD PEOPLE CAN GROW

Want to find the absolute best-adapted plants in your area? *Visit a cemetery!*

When gardeners move on from one garden to another, only the sturdiest of their most attractive plants will likely survive for long. They have to be pretty enough for the next homeowners (no matter their interest or skill) to at least not pull them up and able to survive on no care, no water, and poor pruning.

These same values extend to older cemeteries, where those who care for the graves of their dearly departed set out plants, then give them hit-or-miss care that slowly but surely fades into little or nothing. Decades later, only a few hardy plants survive on their own, in constant hope that they don't get in the way of mowers and string trimmers.

I deliberately cruise around old, established neighborhoods and burial grounds, focusing on what not only survives but still looks good. These plants give me a good baseline of what is truly hardy in a particular area. These are the ones that I recommend to beginner gardeners.

In old cemeteries you will usually find scattered flowering trees, disease-resistant ever-blooming shrubs (including roses, junipers, arborvitae, euonymus, and hollies), and seasonal bulbs and perennials—daffodils, irises, yarrow, native perennial wildflowers, and so much more—even in the dead of winter.

Put a handful of these together in a garden bed, and you will have something that can provide year-round good looks for decades with no care at all.

There are roses that are so tough that even dead people can grow them.

It has become increasingly obvious that native plants, and those imports that can survive on local rainfall and with less fertilizer, are going to be important choices for more gardeners. As water and other resources are becoming increasingly scarce because of over-demand, those plants that can do without will prevail over those that require coddling.

The more tolerance a plant has to benign neglect, the more attractive it will be to gardeners who have less time, or ability, to care for it.

Freedom from Pests

Resistance to pests is a make-or-break quality of pass-along plants. No matter how many qualities a plant has or how easy it is to grow, only a hard-core handful of gardeners will fool with it for long if it has to be sprayed constantly. Roses and zinnias that are resistant to mildew and other leaf diseases are preferred over those that defoliate after every rain. Apples that have twigs killed by fire blight disease won't be appreciated if they rarely bear fruit. Any hibiscus that survives leaf-eating caterpillars will be saved and cherished.

Whether out of environmental concerns or sheer economics, the once-regular use of pesticides—whether synthetic or natural—has come under more intense scrutiny in recent years, with more people vying for plants that simply don't require them.

Plants that are seriously affected by pests are not as likely to be widely grown.

Ease of Propagation

Ease of propagation means plants will be easier to share. It doesn't really matter how well a plant fits the first three characteristics if it takes a lot of propagation skills or special timing to get a "start." Not everyone knows how to graft or has access to a greenhouse mist propagation system.

Pass-along plants are most commonly shared by seed, division of crowns or bulbs, bits of rhizome, rooted cuttings, and offsets (little plants that form on aboveground stems); the best can be propagated nearly any time of the year, regardless of season.

But remember: a lot of plants are so prolific with their progeny that they are considered to be "weeds" (unwanted jewels) by some gardeners. Their seeds, spread by wind, insects, birds, or being stuck on trouser legs, sprout not only where they are wanted, but also in the rain gutter and in neighbors' lawns. Many plants have vigorous underground stolons (like mint) that can torpedo their way out of bounds.

Always keep this in mind when planting something that may be able to escape the garden and become a pest or even an ecological disaster. In fact, you may want to check your state's "invasive plants" lists and regulations—some pretty plants can get, you into hot water.

With a strong new interest in heirloom plants comes more opportunities for plant swaps, seed exchanges, and even commercial sites specializing in rare or all-but-forgotten plants; they provide an important backup against the scary but ever-present specter of a plant "crash" caused by overdependence on a few commercial varieties. Find and support these organizations with your purchases and your excess plants—it's good for everyone.

The easier a plant is to propagate, the more people will share it.

Organized Plant and Seed Saving

In addition to home gardeners saving and sharing plants, there are several larger, better-organized efforts at recognizing and preserving plant diversity. These collective efforts typically search for outstanding varieties of vegetables, fruits, herbs, and flowers that are not widely grown commercially, and that are in danger of being lost forever through lack of attention.

Unfortunately, in the UK and Europe many heritage vegetable varieties (perhaps over two thousand) have been lost since the 1970s; since then, EU laws have been passed to make it illegal to sell any vegetable

A good rule of thumb for getting pass-along plants from other gardeners is the more someone wants to give you, the more you should think twice about accepting.

cultivar that is not on a national list of any EU country. The idea was to help keep varieties true to type and to reduce the dishonesty of seed suppliers selling one seed variety as another. But because some heritage cultivars are not necessarily uniform, and many cultivars have several names coming from different areas or countries, the tests to assess varieties eliminated many seeds from the lists.

Recently there has been a big push in the UK to address these losses by setting up less stringent tests for heritage varieties, to put them on a "B" national list.

Now there are several "seed banks"—public repositories that plant and save heirloom plants and then disburse these plants or seeds to anyone who will use them appropriately such as for studying, breeding (including to find old varieties that are resistant to new diseases), or further distribution.

One such seed bank in the United States is Seed Savers Exchange, based in Decorah, Iowa. Founded in 1975, SSE is a nonprofit, member-supported organization whose network of members saves and shares plants of our garden heritage. These "living legacy" plants have often been passed down through generations of its members.

Seed Savers Exchange, the largest nongovernmental seed bank in the United States, permanently maintains more than 25,000 endangered vegetable, herb, flower, and fruit varieties, most having been brought to North America by members' ancestors who immigrated from Europe, the Middle East, Asia, and other parts of the world. Member farmers and gardeners continually plant or "grow out" the bank's vegetable varieties to keep the stock fresh and viable; the excess is sold to help defray the costs of maintaining the ever-growing collection.

There is no way to give or get a plant from another gardener without having some sort of human contact. Take advantage and have a small conversation. You both might learn something.

Seed Savers Exchange typically looks for antique or heirloom varieties; another seed bank, Seeds of Change, also looks for improved new varieties that can be shared. Started in New Mexico in 1989 by a handful of dedicated gardeners who had the same vision of collecting, growing, and sharing diverse plants, the mission of Seeds of Change is simple: preserving biodiversity and promoting sustainable, organic agriculture.

From its research farm, now located near Santa Fe, the organization's staff continually looks all over the world for new or unique plants to offer. In addition, they create new varieties through traditional plant breeding techniques that bring out unique or improved characteristics or combine desirable traits from existing varieties.

Another premier plant-saving group is the Thomas Jefferson Center for Historic Plants, established in 1987 at Monticello near Charlottesville, Virginia. The center collects, preserves, and distributes historic plant varieties and strives to promote greater appreciation for the origins and evolution of garden plants. The program centers on Thomas Jefferson's horticultural interests and the plants he grew at Monticello, but it covers the broad history of plants cultivated in America by including varieties documented through the nineteenth century and choice North American plants, a group of special interest to Jefferson himself.

There are many other organized efforts as well as commercial ventures run by seriously dedicated individuals who put everything they have into finding, breeding, and sharing plants, especially when it comes to specific kinds of plants. In fact, most plant societies, including antique rose groups, historic bulb collectors, African violet clubs, tomato or pepper specialists, iris and daylily societies, and all the others, are formed and kept going with these goals in mind.

The Pass-Along Plants Project

> Recedite, plebes! Gero rem imperialem.
> *(Stand aside, little people! I am here on official business.)*
>   —anonymous

It is estimated that over 80 percent of the plants most commonly grown are represented by only around forty different species sold in garden centers.

As the whims of horticultural tastes have ebbed and flowed over the centuries, many great garden plants have disappeared, most of them lost forever. However, in spite of the many examples of these long-gone bulbs, perennials, roses, fruits, vegetables, and even native plants, many others have been rescued from the compost heap of fashion and kept alive and shared by garden-variety gardeners and amateur backyard hobbyists.

THE PASS-ALONG PLANTS MANIFESTO

To prevent great garden plants from being lost through neglect by the standardized mass-production practices of large commercial nurseries; to ensure the propagation and planting of highly localized or otherwise endangered flowers, vegetables, edible herbs, and fruits; to reduce pressures on the environment through the use of sustainable garden plants—including garden-worthy natives; to encourage sensory garden education; to make a stand against obsessive worrying about horticultural dogma, which downplays or destroys the essential character of gardening just for the love of it; to protect the right to simple garden pleasures; and to encourage seasonal convivial "plant swaps" to help plants spread more quickly.

Mass-produced plants often flood markets with fewer choices.

Today there are renewed attempts at rediscovering, preserving, maintaining, and spreading such plants by actively encouraging their cultivation for sharing with others. By joining in this effort, Slow Gardeners can help promote the growing of these plants in a sustainable way to help preserve biodiversity in gardens.

The Pass-Along Plants Project aims to rediscover, catalog, describe, and publicize forgotten garden plants that are sustainable enough to thrive in gardens with little or no artificial life support (special fertilizers, pesticides, excessive irrigation). It represents those plants that have fallen by the wayside as fashion and tastes change, or that have been pushed aside by the crush of new hybrids being marketed by modern plant breeders. It encourages the reintroduction of valuable plants that are cherished sustainably—that is, whose culture does not create environmental damage.

The concept of this Pass-Along Plants Project is based loosely on the Slow Food Ark of Taste, which is an international catalog of heritage foods in danger of extinction. The Ark of Taste is designed to preserve at-risk foods that are sustainably produced, unique in taste, and part of a "eco-region"—a large (or sometimes quite small) area with a distinctive culture, one that is affected by climate, landform, soils, and the like.

Similarly, many heirloom flowers, herbs, vegetables, and fruits are in danger of being lost to the whims of fashion and through falling out of favor with the mass production and distribution of the nursery trade.

A Few Selected Pass-Along Plants

No matter where you live—what country, region, state, or even neighborhood—and no matter what your weather or soils are like, you can cruise old neighborhoods and country roads for gardens filled with dozens of commonly grown plants that have been shared by gardeners. Often these plants are grown by many others in the same area, with little or no horticultural upkeep. These are the ones to start with, the back-bone "comfort food" plants that have proven themselves to be worth growing and sharing.

In cool, moist climates you may find more peonies, hollyhocks, rasp-berries, and primulas; in mild-winter areas, gardens are commonly graced with figs, lantana, gardenia, and crape myrtles; in frost-free areas gardeners freely pass around philodendrons, gingers, cold-sensitive flowering vines, and a great variety of palms.

But throughout the gardening world, everywhere you look, you will come across shared daylilies, irises, asters, flowering bulbs, peppers, yarrow, monarda, shrub roses, ornamental grasses, rose of Sharon (althaea), coneflowers, ferns, zinnias, gourds, oregano, and potted plants from all over the tropical world.

These, along with the locally hardy native or otherwise tried-and-true trees, shrubs, and vines that may not be as easily propa-gated and shared, become the backbone of archetypal gardens for each area, lending that oh-so-special "sense of place" that makes people long for wherever "back home" may be.

Because of the huge diversity of heirloom garden plants, any list will certainly seem to be random. Examples include the super-hot Jalokia pepper, the heirloom 'Moon and Stars' watermelon, a perennial lychnis with large orange flowers, brown and green strains of cotton, heat-tolerant 'Festiva Maxima' peony for Southern gardeners, and *Franklinia,* a beautiful native flow-ering tree now extinct in the wild but thriving in gardens.

Sedums are cherished pass-along plants all over the world.

Plants included in the following lists are intended to be culturally or historically linked to a specific region, locality, ethnicity, or traditional garden practice. Plants that meet these criteria can be examined by well-known garden enthusiasts, including avid home gardeners, botanic garden and historic plant-collection curators, and university researchers who specialize in heirloom plants.

The 'Moon and Stars' watermelon has been saved from extinction by home gardeners.

Criteria for Selection to the List

To be included on this list, plants should:

• Possess garden value— beauty, taste, fragrance, attractiveness for wildlife, historic significance and/or links to a specific region or ethnic group, etc. (the more values the better).

• Be of good garden quality—acceptable in most garden settings.

• Be well acclimated to local soils, climate, and weather.

• Be environmentally sustainable without routine irrigation or excessive fertilization.

• Be relatively free of major pests—not dependent on pesticides for beauty of production.

• Be easy to propagate by seed, cutting, or division, for sharing among a wide range of gardeners with diverse gardening skills.

Note: Hybrid plants can be included in this list, but not those that are trademarked or otherwise not available for free sharing between gardeners.

Universally Grown Pass-Along Plants

(*most climates*)

- Daylily
- Iris
- Artemisia
- Sedum
- Yarrow
- Ferns
- Canna
- Yucca
- Mints
- Painted arum
- Ornamental grasses
- Phlox
- Amsonia
- Chives
- Sempervivum
- Rosemary
- Saponaria
- Rose
- Peppers
- Tomatoes
- Althaea (rose of Sharon)

Painted arum is a pass-along plant in most regions of the country.

Heirloom geraniums are often shared among gardeners in cool climates.

Cool-Climate Pass-Along Plants

(*Pacific Northwest, Midwest, Mid-Atlantic, New England, southern Canada, United Kingdom, northern Europe*)

- Hosta
- Peony
- Solomon's seal
- Rhubarb
- Hollyhocks
- Hellebore
- Monarda
- Crocosmia
- Astilbe
- Geranium
- Pelargonium
- Raspberry

Four o'clocks are a classic shared plant in warm climates.

Warm-Climate Pass-Along Plants

(*Southern California, Southwest, Southeast, Florida, Mediterranean*)

- Ruellia
- Liriope
- Purple heart (*Tradescantia pallida*)
- Four o'clocks
- Aspidistra
- Elephant ears
- Agave
- Obedient plant (*Physostegia*)
- Alstroemeria
- Society garlic
- Fig
- Peppers

Tropical Pass-Along Perennials

(*universally grown in containers, even where they can be grown outside*)

- Sansevieria
- Aloe vera
- Begonias
- Airplane plant (*Chlorophytum*)
- Night-blooming cereus (*Hylocereus*)
- Pencil cactus (*Euphorbia tirucalli*)
- Asparagus fern
- Rubber tree
- Chinese hibiscus
- African violets
- Dracaenas
- Orchids
- Bromeliads
- Philodendrons

Sansevieria is one of the most popular shared tropical potted plants.

Garden Convivality: Organizing a Plant Swap

My mother quit the garden club because they stopped swapping plants at the meetings.
   —Eudora Welty

Growing plants may be a major goal of gardening, but sharing is a major opportunity. Usually it is done informally, person to person, over or under the fence, but there is also a way to share the wealth through easily organized plant swaps.

A plant swap is a great way for gardeners to mix it up with others, in a safe setting—a good time with no strings attached.

Some communities have areas set aside seasonally where gardeners can leave excess or unwanted plants for others to pick up. Others have regularly scheduled meetings where gardeners bring plants to swap on the spot with other gardeners.

Though the easiest and most efficient plant swaps are those with the fewest rules, a few guidelines can make things flow more smoothly.

The hardest to enforce is that of limiting the number of plants individual gardeners can bring to swap. Extra plants can be shared informally after the swap, but it's best to keep the number of plants entered in the formal swap to just one or two. This reduces the likelihood of someone bringing in a lot of one kind of plant, or junky plants that are not worth sharing, and expecting better plants in return.

It's a good idea to start a plant swap in the right frame of mind, with the announcement that the swap is not a way to get lots of new plants, but a place to meet

Local plant swaps are where nonjoiner gardeners meet to share heirloom plants.

like-minded gardeners and see the incredible diversity of people and plants that are begging to get together later and share more.

If possible during the advertisement for the swap, ask people to bring only ready-to-grow plants that "non-gardeners" can grow: avoid wilted, newly dug, bare-root, or pest-ridden plants, dormant bulbs, and those specimens that most reasonable gardeners would consider to be serious pest plants (one person's wildflower is another's worst weed).

Try to have someone inspect each plant before the swap, to make sure weeds, insects, or diseases are not being swapped along with the treasured plant.

To organize the swap, have a numbered stick or piece of paper attached to each plant in the swap, and put a matching number in a box to be pulled later. When the swap begins, everyone who has entered a plant can pull a number from the box.

Whatever number gets pulled, the plant with the corresponding number is the one that is received—no matter if the plant is wanted or not. No matter if the person already has a similar plant or even if the person actually brought that plant to the swap. The real swapping goes on informally after the numbers are all pulled and the plants are all divvied up.

Lastly, because some curious souls always show up without plants to swap, it's a good idea to have a few extras on hand to share afterward.

Believe it or not, this works pretty well.

Plant (and Gardener) Diversity

Plants—the backbone of any garden, coming in all sizes, shapes, and uses—represent more than just beauty or food; they serve as outlets for our hobbies, our passions, our scientific curiosities, even our compulsions (as with plant collectors).

Slow Gardeners, who appreciate modern plant hybrids and antique heirloom varieties alike, also come in every form and fashion, from those who just love fragrant old roses to those who are driven to develop ever-more interesting forms of fragrant old roses to those who have a passion for developing the skills needed to grow a perfect rose.

And though we all love to share either our plants or our passions, or both, with anyone who wanders by with an admiring eye, most of us are perfectly content to just putter around, doing what we do just for the satisfaction of having done it well.

Slow Gardening is about getting the most out of our garden efforts—which usually means getting the best plants to begin with, and growing and displaying them well.

Above all, let's never forget that plants are living, breathing creatures that, when they come into our gardens as guests, should be treated as such, and never taken for granted.

One of the best ways we can preserve great, locally adapted heirloom plants is, to paraphrase Louisiana food and cultural preservationist Poppy Tooker, "Grow it, to save it." And then share it.

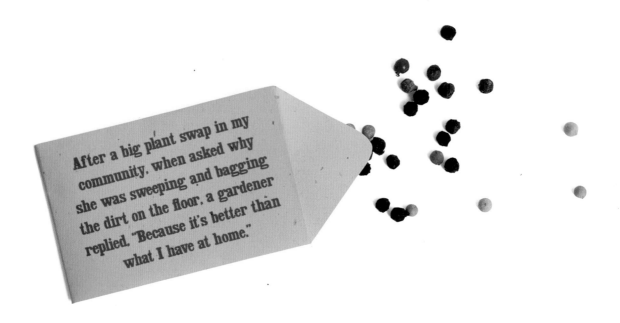

After a big plant swap in my community, when asked why she was sweeping and bagging the dirt on the floor, a gardener replied, "Because it's better than what I have at home."

CHAPTER FIVE
Nuts and Bolts: Universal Garden Practices

No greater thing is created suddenly, any more than a bunch of grapes or a fig; if you tell me that you desire a fig, I answer you that there must be time. Let it first blossom, then bear fruit, then ripen.
— Epictetus

For the most part, the practice of Slow Gardening is simply good gardening, which encompasses a lot of basic, commonly shared knowledge and skills.

And Slow Gardeners tend to look for the best (and hopefully sustainable) results with the least effort. The main thing is, we just try to enjoy what we do, as we do it. After all, it's the trip, not the destination, that is so relaxing.

But to be perfectly blunt, there isn't a whole lot that you *have* to do to be a pretty successful gardener. For the vast majority of gardeners down through history, there have been only three basic rules needed to grow most plants: dig wide holes, set plants in green side up, and, if they need it, water them a few times during the first few months. The rest is what I call horticultural finesse.

Regardless of landscape style or other personal preferences, everyday garden chores, from choosing and putting plants in the ground to dealing with the aftermath of bad weather, are done pretty much the same by all gardeners everywhere, with mostly minor variations.

So, how do we actually pull off the feat we call gardening? As a horticulturist and longtime garden teacher, I can "wax eloquent" on most

Gardening should be simple enough for even a child.

aspects of landscaping and gardening, so much so that I almost hate to get started reading, much less writing, about the "nuts and bolts" of gardening—so same old, same old.

Yet, as a gardener, I know that most of my tasks are just that: repetitive series of actions that stretch out, season after season, year after year, until I move on to something else. These are things that simply need doing—and understanding is the first step.

Still, there are many extra steps we can take, plus countless stylistic or climate-driven variations—more than enough to keep the most serious gardener in search of better ways to get through the seasons.

Not a Lot of How-To

I'm the ultimate busy/tired/gone/lazy/other-stuff-to-do kind of gardener. But Slow Gardening has room for folks who want to get the very most out of their efforts—be it a perfect lawn or hybridizing the next new "must have" plant—and who find it interesting to see how far they can take gardening.

For them there are untold thousands of websites, blogs, books, local experts, and plant societies for networking and sharing—lots of easy-to-find resources for anyone wanting more esoteric details.

Meanwhile, regardless of interests, abilities, or style, if you are like any other gardener, your bookshelf is already groaning under the weight of at least two or three more gardening how-to books than you really need. Most do a great job of covering the same basics of choosing, planting, and caring for various plants, all of which is the basis of being a good gardener, but most of which covers the same ground as every other garden book.

So, this chapter is a somewhat oversimplified, in-a-nutshell version of the same old stuff, done pretty much the same way by most gardeners, with small twists I have gleaned from decades of gardening on my own and working with fellow gardeners all over the world.

You won't find a lot of horticultural instruction here, for two reasons: it is covered more thoroughly in nearly every other garden book—or online—and, to be truthful, most hardy plants simply don't need a lot of fuss. Most require only two acts on your part: dig a wide hole, and plant them green-side up.

Any more detail than this can get tedious, except to hard-core horticulturists—and this book is not for them anyway!

Let me remind you that I honestly believe that both the high-end horticultural approach, as taken by serious hobbyists such as plant collectors and intense lovers of lawns, and the less-driven "just get 'er done" attitude of weekend dabblers in search of a little exercise, sunshine, and peace of mind work equally well for different personality types.

The Slow approach is to find and follow what best suits you, your interests and abilities, your situation (including family and neighbors), and your climate.

Hopefully my simplified "deconstructionist" take on gardening chores will work for you, too.

First Things First: Weather Matters

Spring is both father and mother to us.
   —Swainson's *Handbook of Weather Folk-Lore*

Where you live strongly affects how well you can pull off growing things easily.

No matter where you live it seems as if, the gardening conditions are guaranteed to be different—usually dramatically so—from those found just a few miles away. And nobody understands us. Tomatoes always grew better where we used to live, never where we currently find ourselves. As garden philosopher Henry Mitchell put it, "Where there are great gardens, there are great heartaches."

I have gardened on four continents and on all three coasts of the United States, and believe me, nobody has it easy. From the heat and suffocating humidity of the Gulf Coast to the chilly nights of arid Southern California, and on into the deep freezes of the Upper Midwest and New England, we all have our challenges.

Even the fabled English gardeners have to contend with miserable weather during a big part of the year; and sunny Florida—on top of hurricanes, which can hurl bowling balls a hundred yards—has a predictable drought every winter.

The overriding consensus for easy gardening in all these places? *Plant what grows best, and forget the rest.*

There are a few natural considerations that largely determine what kind of garden you can have most easily. Hard constraints include weather, temperature ranges, availability of sunlight, and your particular soil type, which often dictate the kinds of plants that will survive outside and how much time you can stand being outside yourself. Softer influences range from the amount of time you have to garden, your interests, and your physical abilities to the garden styles and attitudes of neighbors (including neighborhood restrictions and covenants, which may limit or prohibit certain landscape styles).

If you want to go above and beyond those "given" parameters, you will have to modify them or garden around them. But knowledge comes before understanding.

You can only support so many plants for so long with artificial life support, and only a few hard-core nutty gardeners will continue, year after year, to cover plants that can't take the weather.

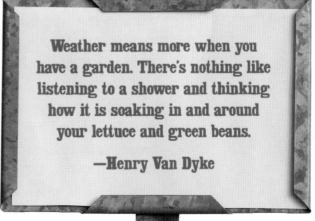

Weather means more when you have a garden. There's nothing like listening to a shower and thinking how it is soaking in and around your lettuce and green beans.

—Henry Van Dyke

Still, horticulturists come up with all sorts of schemes to help guide us—floating row covers, anti-desiccant sprays, drip irrigation, even probes connected to our computers that "tell" us when our plants need attention. These are fantastic tools for folks who want to push the envelope, and in many cases they can mean the difference between success and failure.

Meanwhile, the real answers are right around the corner, in the uncelebrated yards of garden-variety gardeners who simply dig in and plant stuff, and, if it fails, they try again, then give up and move on to something else that is easier to grow in their climate. For now, let's look at a few of the more important considerations of how where you live affects your garden.

Climate

I've lived in a good climate, and it bores the hell out of me. I like weather rather than climate.
—John Steinbeck

A large part of your gardening happiness is dependent on your accepting, if not outright getting used to, the climate where you live. Nobody likes a complainer, especially when everyone around is in the same boat! There's not much you can do about it anyway, other than move.

Climate is a given for most folks. But it's still worth giving a nod to what is, for most gardeners around the world, the overriding factor in what and when to plant. In most areas the climate is reasonably predictable from year to year, though lots of people notice gradual changes over time based on many years of observation. Plus, there are always factors like atmospheric currents (the jet stream) and oceanic cycles (El Niño versus La Niña) that can steer storms toward or away from a region, meaning that some years will be hotter, wetter, or drier than average.

There's nothing more frustrating than moving to a new area and butting heads with people who have learned over many years to go with the flow of their local climate.

Gardeners in cool climates have more of a sense of urgency to get stuff done in a short growing season, and they learn how to enjoy indoor or greenhouse activities during inclement weather; whereas gardeners in hotter or tropical climates tend to take their time because there really isn't a big rush, and besides, it's too hot to move quickly anyway.

Terroir was originally a French term used in wine and coffee appreciation circles, to denote the special characteristics of geography, soils, and climate that bestow distinctive qualities upon a particular food product. In Slow Gardening terms, *terroir* can be very loosely translated as "a sense of place," which is embodied in the sum of the effects that our local environment has on most of what we do.

So take your time: study not only *what* people in your area do, but *why*. Maybe it will save you from unnecessary anxiety or grief in your own garden.

By the way, some folks move back and forth between different parts of a country—or even between different countries—during various

Gardeners modify their environments to grow plants in difficult settings.

seasons. They can be easily frustrated when trying to keep similar plants alive in dramatically different climates. In these circumstances, the easy satisfaction of enjoying one-size-fits-all gardens in different settings is usually outweighed by the interesting phenomenon of gardening in different cultures.

For example, while I love the subtropical plants that thrive in the heat and humidity of my Mississippi homeland, I don't pine for them when I spend a summer in the western Midlands of England, where I savor the cool-climate fruits and flowers that wouldn't last a month back home.

"Snowbirds" from the northern United States who overwinter in Florida should leave their lilacs and peonies back home, and Southerners who escape the heat by staying in New England summers would be well advised to leave their okra down South.

The Slow Gardener can turn this "going with the flow" approach to his or her advantage, as opposed to always playing catch-up or being forced to nursemaid a bunch of unhappy plants.

Plant Hardiness Zone Maps: No Promises

One way horticulturists have tried to address climate differences is by delineating various "plant hardiness zones" that detail various average local conditions and labeling plants according to which zones they will likely grow best in (or at any rate where they will survive and tolerate the conditions).

Many outstanding gardeners will tell you that these maps are perfectly fine and useful—no problem. In fact, many gardeners simply won't buy a book that isn't written for their specific part of the world, based solely on plant hardiness zones.

But the truth is, to many new gardeners the maps are confusing, and most experienced old hands know that following the zone information to the letter offers no guarantee of success.

Besides, all gardeners sooner or later try their luck with plants that are known to be borderline hardy in their area. It's just human nature to want to push the limits.

One problem with the maps is that they are based on averages, not realities. An old quote taken from *The Old Farmer's Almanac* goes, "Put one foot on a hot stove and the other one on a block of ice, and the 'average' should feel just about right." This is particularly frustrating when considering the recent changes in climate: whether they are short- or long-term in duration, they are real; growing seasons *are* a bit longer than they used to be, winters are milder, summers are harsher. Plant zone maps cannot realistically keep up with these important shifts.

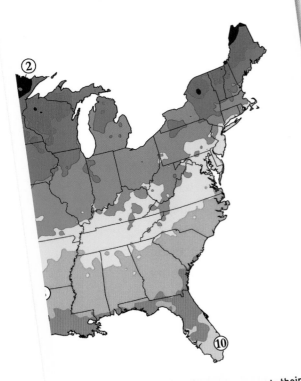

Climate zone maps are useful but often narrow in their application.

Besides, the charts don't take everything into consideration; as they say in Florida, "What thrives in the Panhandle may fry in the Keys." Me, I won't be satisfied until a zone map is devised that includes temperatures both high and low, rainfall through all the year, humidity, wind, soil type (including acidity or alkalinity), and my current attitude.

So use zone maps with a grain of salt and as general guidelines for selecting plants of which you are unsure.

Meanwhile, choose plants for your garden based on the ones that are growing all around you, regardless of what the zone maps predict.

Watering Wisely

Water does not necessarily equal love; too much may not be a good thing.

Plants, like people, are made mostly out of water. But for most plants, too much water, whether from rainfall or irrigation, can overwhelm roots, effectively drowning the plants. And too much water leaches nutrients from the soil—especially from highly soluble chemical fertilizers, wasting money and potentially polluting ground and surface waters.

We simply have to water every now and then, or do without some great plants. But with the exception of newly set-out plants and potted plants, daily or even twice-weekly watering is not only not necessary, but downright wasteful (and people notice). A garden hose can spew up to six hundred gallons of precious water an hour!

It is therefore crucial to understand that area water patterns affect how and what you plant, and to have a plan for how you can get around the inevitable shortfalls or excesses.

There are no hard or reliable rules for watering plants, just a lot of loose advice. Some plants, particularly natives and others that have become well adapted to your climate, can survive on rainfall alone. You can see this by simply observing older gardens in small towns and along country roads. "Drought-tolerant" means that a plant can go weeks or months without supplemental water, just surviving on rainfall alone—but this is nearly impossible for the vast majority of landscape plants.

Potted plants, summer annuals, and a nicely maintained lawn need watering fairly often, but well-established trees and shrubs barely need any water at all; in fact, watering woody plants and perennials too frequently keeps their roots shallow and needy. While some plants can tolerate deep freezes, some get damaged during sunny, windy winter days without snow cover to protect the soil from drying out.

DRIP IRRIGATION

My home garden is mostly self-sustaining, in terms of water, but my container-grown herbs and vegetables can dry out quickly, especially in hot or windy weather—and I am often gone for days or weeks at a time, with no one to care for my plants. So I use a simple but special setup called drip irrigation.

Drip irrigation is a dramatic way to reduce the amount of water used in the garden—an increasingly important consideration, especially in dry climates and other areas where water is considered a dwindling resource.

Most systems simply use small tubes to deliver water directly to the base of individual plants or into containers. The flexible "spaghetti" tubes are attached at one end to a hose or other water supply; the loose end has a small "emitter" inserted that allows only a small amount of water to drip out (usually one or two gallons an hour).

My system is run by an inexpensive timer that turns the water on for an hour or two at a time, every two or three days (depending on the weather and rainfall). It saves water, and it saves me from worrying about whether my plants will still be there when I get home.

Still, water is important to good gardens. What to do? Here are a few tried-and-true water-saving tips:

- Raise your lawn mower height a notch or two, and feed grass lightly with slow-release organic fertilizers; these help the grass grow steadily without needing as much water.
- Water lawns in the early morning or early evening to minimize evaporation and waste, and water no more than once or twice a week in the summer—if that often. (*Note:* Most turfgrasses, when allowed to go dry during hot spells, simply go dormant, and they will green up again after a good soaking rain.)
- Lose most, if not all, of the lawn. Landscape largely with locally adapted, drought-tolerant plants, trees, and ornamental grasses.
- Group plants together based on their water needs.
- Mulch to retain moisture and reduce weeds, and feed the soil.
- Water at the base of plants, not overhead, to reduce evaporation.
- Water deeply, not frequently; soaker hoses and drip irrigation are more efficient and less troublesome for disease-prone plants than overhead watering. (*Hint:* Water twice, an hour or so apart, to give the first watering time to soak in; the second watering really pushes it down deep. Sometimes I even water my plants after a light rain, to maximize the effect.)
- Place a shut-off valve on the end of your hose to control the flow and use only what you need.
- Install a rain sensor switch in your irrigation system to override it when it rains.
- Build or buy a rain barrel or other water collection system attached to the downspout of your roof. (My own front porch, designed to funnel rain from my roof into a large cistern, "harvests" nearly 300 gallons of water every time my roof gets just one inch of rainfall!)

• Design a "rain garden" that collects water in a low area during excess rain, and plant it with wetland plants that tolerate rainy and dry seasons, like those found in most low-lying areas or ditches in your part of the world. This is a very effective and attractive way to slow down, collect, and use natural rainfall.

Plants

Let's face it, most of us consider plants to be the most important parts of a garden. Yet given identical settings and the same selection to choose from, no two gardeners would likely pick the same kinds of plants to grow.

This is because, to a smart gardener, plants can almost be afterthoughts to a well-designed landscape, as interchangeable as pie fillings to a baker.

What we want to grow may not be the most important consideration here (remember *climate*?), yet there are often similar selections—especially when it comes to growing plants just for beauty or ornament—that are similar in size, shape, form, color, or other attributes.

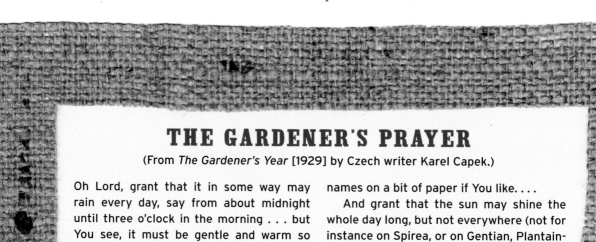

THE GARDENER'S PRAYER
(From *The Gardener's Year* [1929] by Czech writer Karel Capek.)

Oh Lord, grant that it in some way may rain every day, say from about midnight until three o'clock in the morning . . . but You see, it must be gentle and warm so that it can soak in; grant that at the same time it would not rain on Campion, Alyssum, Helianthemum, Lavender and other plants which You in Your infinite wisdom know are drought-loving plants. . . . I will write their names on a bit of paper if You like. . . .

And grant that the sun may shine the whole day long, but not everywhere (not for instance on Spirea, or on Gentian, Plantain-lily or Rhododendron), and not too much . . . that there be plenty of dew and little wind, enough worms, no plant lice and snails, no mildew, and that once a week thin, liquid manure and guano may fall from Heaven.

For example, where it may be too hot to grow great lilac shrubs, substitute crape myrtle; where apples may not thrive, try figs; keep in mind that ripe sweet peppers are not only easier to grow in cool climates than citrus trees, but, pound for pound, they also contain more vitamins.

For most landscape and garden uses, the most important types of plants are long-lived "woody" trees, shrubs, and vines (including fruit plants); herbaceous perennials, which can live for many years; and one-shot annuals (including most vegetables). Most gardeners all over the world, including in tropical climates, but especially those who live in climates that freeze part of the year, also enjoy keeping a few tropical plants in pots. And a growing number of gardeners are enjoying simple water gardens with at least a few aquatic plants.

More specifics on the different types of plants can be found in chapter 4.

Soil: Modified Dirt

Horticulturists and trained gardeners refer to the stuff in which plants grow as "soil"—but everyone knows what dirt is. Actually, both terms are correct, both being based on ancient words that describe basically the same stuff. To me, soil is "improved dirt." But to keep things calm—you'd be surprised at how easily otherwise intelligent people can become alienated over mere words—I will refer to it all as soil.

Growing healthy plants starts with healthy soil. Period. This includes learning what kind of soil your garden has, and amending it if needed to grow a wide variety of plants.

There are no good or bad soils, just different types. Most are mineral-based, and (excuse the pun) lumped into clay, sand, loam, silt, and all sorts of mixtures of them all. These terms are based on the texture of the mineral content—the size of individual particles and how well they bind together.

While rocky or sandy soils are mostly loose and well drained and do not hold moisture or nutrients very well, in general the smaller, plate-like particles of clay soils tend to stick together and hold moisture and nutrients, but they do not allow water or air to penetrate as quickly.

Soil is what horticulturists call "modified native dirt."

Mix enough sandy soil with clay soil, and you should get a blend that has the attributes of both—enough sand will loosen a clay soil, while clay firms up sandy soils.

Of course these are gross overgeneralizations! But they work for most gardeners.

An ideal garden soil will be loose enough to allow water and air to penetrate easily and percolate fairly quickly yet have enough "pore space" between particles to allow excess water to drain away and pull fresh air into the soil. Yet it will hold enough moisture to keep plant roots from drying out too quickly.

In addition, soil particles should hold on to nutrients as long as possible, to keep plants growing steadily without a lot of supplemental fertilizing.

Organic Matter

All over the world, good gardeners know that the single most important way to improve soil is through the addition of decomposed organic matter—aged manure, decomposed leaves, bark, or even old plants, or "cover crops" grown specifically to be dug into the native dirt and allowed to decompose awhile.

Store-bought organic matter is readily available in all garden centers, but you can easily make your own by piling various kinds of fresh material such as leaves, grass clippings, spent flowers and plants that have been pulled up, shredded cardboard and paper, plant-based kitchen scraps including coffee grounds and filters, and even eggshells. This practice is called *composting,* and it dates back to whenever the first gardener added a handful of leaf mold to a planting hole.

Compost: Grow Your Own

In addition to manure and other kinds of organic matter, gardeners can buy bagged compost at any garden center, or perhaps get it free from municipal leaf collection points. But the Slow way of doing it is to make your own!

Too much has been written and said about composting. It makes me tired just thinking about all I'm supposed to do: small particle sizes, correct carbon–nitrogen ratio, thermophilic bacteria, exact bin sizes, turning and aerating, and all the rest of that stuff!

Yet, as anyone with a leaf pile will attest, composting just *happens*. Naturally.

Pardon the deconstructionism, but all a compost bin is is a fenced-in leaf pile. Takes a while to do its thing, but it does happen, usually within weeks or months. And once you get

Simple bins can be used to organize leaf piles into compost systems.

started, it is easy to keep it going by adding new stuff as the old finished compost is "harvested."

As Joe Keyser, former head of research at the American Horticulture Society and now known as "America's Compost King," puts it, "There are only two rules for composting: Stop throwing that stuff away, and pile it up somewhere."

The rest is finesse. If you want to get in a race with someone, go online, or call your county extension service office for a handout, and you will quickly find a few tips for speeding up the process. The easiest ones to remember are, in order of importance:

- To the carbon-rich "brown" stuff (fallen leaves, decaying manure, etc.) that makes up the bulk of a compost

There are only two rules for composting: Stop throwing that stuff away, and pile it up somewhere.
—Joe Keyser, "America's Compost King"

pile, mix in a little nitrogen-rich "green" stuff, including grass clippings and vegetable scraps, even weeds; where not enough green stuff is available, substitute a little bit of nitrogen fertilizer.

- Chop big pieces into smaller pieces.
- Turn the pile occasionally to mix and fluff or aerate it (air is necessary for good bacterial activity).
- Keep the pile moist, but not wet (moisture is also needed by good bacteria).

If you don't have or don't want a compost bin or two, at least make a leaf pile somewhere, and dig out of it as you need to. But really, the most important thing about composting is not how fast you can make it; forget the rules—just do it!

Vermicomposting, a variation on composting using worms, usually in boxes kept indoors, is easy and provides a low-odor way to recycle kitchen scraps and newspapers.

While there are any number of commercially available vermicomposting boxes and kits, I use a large, inexpensive plastic box with a tight-fitting lid (the kind most folks use to store sweaters or other seasonal clothing). After slicing a few narrow ventilation holes in the top and upper sides of the box, I fill it with hand-shredded newspapers (only black-and-white print—no slick ads or colored paper), barely moisten it, then add a cup or two of finely chopped kitchen scraps (fruit and vegetables, coffee grounds, eggshells, but no oil or meat).

To this I add special "red wiggler" worms—small, reddish brown tropical worms (available at bait shops or online) that consume organic debris quickly at indoor temperatures. Then I close the top firmly to keep the night-roaming worms in the bin.

Within days the food scraps are gone, along with a good bit of the shredded paper. I add more of each as needed, covering fresh scraps with more paper. If the bin gets too wet, I fold in dry paper to absorb excess moisture.

SOIL PH: A BIG DEAL OVER NOTHING?

Soil pH—the measure of acidity or alkalinity of a soil—definitely influences plant growth by affecting fertilizer availability and even whether or not certain beneficial soil microbes reproduce and thrive. But in my opinion it is often exaggerated. Truth is, soil pH can rarely be changed appreciably, or for very long. And ups and downs in conditions caused by too much tinkering are worse for plants than nothing at all.

Using soil tests to determine the correct amounts, farmers and serious hobby gardeners—who need to pay close attention to all aspects of their soils—occasionally add crushed limestone to acidic soils, which can affect the pH for a while. But nothing much practical can be done to amend alkaline soils, because acid-forming materials don't really work that well unless they can be worked into the soil.

However, fertilizing carefully and regularly, working lots of organic matter —compost or "green manure" cover crops—

into gardens or flower beds can work pretty well to compensate for a moderately off-kilter soil pH.

Am I saying you don't need to have your soil tested, or worry at all about soil pH? Absolutely not! Farmers and horticulturists who make their living from growing crops, and intense hobbyists trying to get the most out of their plants or lawns, need all the tools they can get. Plus, some plants, like blueberries and azaleas, grow much better in a more acidic soil; making adjustments for them cannot be done accurately without a soil test.

But the truth is, most garden-variety gardeners never really think about, much less fool with these things—and they do pretty well.

If you want to know your soil's pH for sure, call your university extension service to arrange for a soil test—and be sure to call them back when you get the computerized results and need help interpreting them!

Red wiggler worms turn newspaper and kitchen scraps into high-quality compost—indoors.

To "harvest" the nutrient-rich vermi-compost—which I use on potted plants and around herbs and vegetables—I scatter fresh scraps over the surface, wait overnight for the worms to come up to feed, then gently lift them into another container while I dig out the rich brown compost and start the whole process over.

The Myth of the Five-Dollar Hole

Back in my college days I was taught that "it is better to put a fifty-cent plant in a five-dollar hole, than a five-dollar plant in a fifty-cent hole." This meant adding organic matter to the soil when setting out trees, shrubs, perennials, and other flowers, which was often considered crucial to early plant survival.

However, in the long run we learned we were overdoing things, to the point where a lot of plants simply did not grow good roots outside of the over-amended holes, and their roots simply rotted in wet weather or dried out too quickly in dry weather.

The current thinking is that a lot of plants grow best in just plain native dirt. This helps plants get used to the soil around them as quickly as possible. Now landscapers add little or no organic matter to the planting hole, preferring to select plants that grow well in the native soil.

In most gardens, especially where unusual plants with finicky roots are preferred, a moderate approach—somewhere between the two extremes of native dirt and completely amended soil—usually works best.

To figure out how much organic matter to add, think "crackers in chili"—a bowl of chili usually doesn't need any crackers at all, but a handful of crumbled crackers can fluff it up and cool it down; adding more than a handful, though, just turns it into mush.

Similarly, dig your soil a solid shovel's depth, turning it upside-down and chopping up the clumps. Spread over the area a layer of organic material (compost, manure, potting soil, finely ground bark, whatever), and stir it into the native soil.

How much to add? My personal rule of thumb is:

- For trees and hardy shrubs, add little or no organic matter.
- For shrubs with fibrous roots (blueberries, azaleas, etc.), hybrid roses, most herbaceous perennials, and other plants that need extra moisture in dry seasons or better drainage in wet spells, add a one- or two-inch layer of organic matter and work it thoroughly into the native soil.
- For raised beds with herbs, vegetables, and other fast-growing but short-lived annuals, add a three- or four-inch layer, and work it in well.

Mulches Make a Difference

You don't spit into the wind, you don't tug on Superman's cape, and you don't scrimp on those mulches.
    —H. Randall Smith, American horticulturist

You can make a dramatic improvement in your soil if, after planting, you cover the soil surface with a "blanket" of porous material, preferably something that breaks down over time to improve the soil underneath. This is one of the most important things a gardener can do to help plants get adjusted and thrive over the long haul.

Mulches, which can be organic (bark, leaves, compost, straw, etc.) or inorganic (gravel, sand, crushed glass, paving stones), are simply materials that cover the soil surface completely yet allow air, water, and fertilizers to pass through to get to plant roots.

Plastic sheeting and other synthetic landscape fabrics, some of which can help keep weeds from growing (at least for a while), often interfere with these important characteristics; most gardeners prefer to use natural mulches of leaves, pine straw, compost, or bark, which "feed" and enrich the soil as they decompose or are eaten and taken deep around roots by earthworms.

Organic mulches protect soil and neaten the garden.

Mulches provide several important benefits to soil and plants. They:

- Moderate soil temperatures in both hot and cold weather, and from day to night.
- Conserve moisture, especially on windy days,when soil can quickly "wick" dry.
- Reduce weed growth, particularly from seeds that need sun or soil contact to sprout.
- Cover ground where plants may not be desired (when you're eliminating part of the lawn, during establishment of new planting areas, or under trees and shrubs where little else will grow).
- Help control erosion, especially on slopes.
- "Feed" the soil as the mulch decomposes (organic mulches only).
- Look good—many mulches are highly ornamental and can be chosen accordingly.
- "Connect" the bases of trees and shrubs, reducing the amount of mowing needed.

Spread mulch evenly over the root area of plants—don't simply pile it up around trunks and stems like an ant mound or volcano, or the mulch may shed water away from plants, keep stems too wet and create conditions favorable for diseases, or provide a good habitat for destructive insects or even bark-gnawing rodents.

How much mulch to use? My general rule of thumb is to apply just enough to completely but barely cover the soil surface, then add that much more to allow for settling. (*Note:* It takes more pine straw to cover the soil than bark mulch or compost.) Then plan to add even more mulch as needed, as the original material settles or decomposes.

Planting

Putting plants in the ground requires little more than understanding what "green side up" means; still, there are a few guidelines that most gardeners master quickly. For the most part, they involve how deep to set plants and what to do afterward to help them get off to a solid start for long-term healthy growth.

With the exception of tomatoes and other vines, which can grow new roots up and down stems when buried a little too deep, and iris, whose ropelike rhizome can rot if planted even a little too deep, most trees, shrubs, and flowers grow best when set into the ground so the "crown" of the plant—that part right above where roots start growing—is level with the soil surface around the planting site.

If the soil is very loose or highly amended with compost or other organic material, the plant may sink a little over time; plants in those soil conditions can be set a little higher to allow for settling.

After planting, make sure the soil is slightly compacted around the roots, to remove underground air spaces or "pockets"; this is usually easily done by firming the soil with your hands or foot. Water thoroughly to further settle soil around the roots, then cover the planting area with a good layer of mulch.

Potted Plants

Plants grown in pots are utterly dependent on the care given by gardeners. Some are more tolerant of neglect than others, but all can quickly become victims that either die miserably or simply look bad (in which case they may be better off on the compost pile).

Pots should be durable enough to withstand weather and moving around, and, with the exception of water gardens in containers, most require holes to allow extra water to drain out during rainy periods or after heavy watering. Decorative pots can have smaller pots within them, to be removed for drainage after watering.

Repotting should be done when plants have been in the same worn-out potting soil for years or when the plant has gotten too big for its pot.

Most potted plants are tropical in origin but can thrive if three basic environmental needs—right temperature range, good light, and right humidity—are met. Light requirements range from direct sunshine through a clear window to low light that is still easy to read by. No need to get technical—just remember that while some plants will survive for months in very dim areas, most do best either right in or right beside a bright window.

Though many tropical cacti and succulents do fine without it, humidity is important for many tropical plants, including ferns, African violets, and orchids. At the very least, make sure the plants are not kept in the direct draft from an air conditioner or heater, both of which pull water from the leaves of plants more quickly than they can replace it via roots and stems. Cluster plants close together to create a humid "microclimate."

The right temperature range is crucial for most tropical plants. Most do fine in the same temperatures that are most comfortable for humans, though many—like us—will tolerate occasional rises (to around 100°F) or brief dips into more chilly conditions.

Good location aside, potted plants also have cultural needs. How you take care of your plants can determine the difference between their thriving and merely surviving. Water, fertilizer, and occasional repotting are about all these selections need, though an occasional bout of pests may need to be dealt with.

Watering "as needed" is the rule of thumb. Too wet is worse than too dry. To know when plants need watering, stick your finger in the potting soil or lift the pot to check for weight. *Never* water just on a regular schedule, because variations in environmental conditions, plant type, pot size, potting-soil type, and the amount of fertilizer used will cause plants to grow at different rates and require water in varying amounts.

Fertilizer is plant food, and while many potted plants can survive for years on just water alone, that's being abusive. Yet overfeeding can cause problems—too much fertilizer can be more damaging than too little. Because the directions on containers indicate the absolute highest application amounts the manufacturer can legally get away with, I recommend using only about half the recommended amount, which is plenty adequate for most plants.

Pests, including spider mites, mealy bugs, and scale insects, can be annoying, but they can usually be controlled by pruning out the

FELDER'S PERSONAL POTTING-SOIL RECIPE

In college I did research on various potting-soil mixes and came up with an all-purpose blend that holds up a long time, keeps plants upright in the pots, stays moist without staying wet, and holds nutrients so they don't wash out too quickly. It is easy to make and inexpensive; I mix it on the driveway and store it in a plastic garbage can.

Ingredients: one part cheap potting soil and one part finely ground bark mulch. That's it. The bark allows good water and air penetration; the potting soil holds moisture and nutrients. If a plant needs more drainage, I add more bark (or sometimes the white crunchy material called perlite);
if it needs more water-holding capacity, I add compost or peat moss. There are some water-retention gels that work quite well for helping small pots and hanging baskets hold water longer between soakings, but a very small amount goes a long, long way—don't overdo it when mixing them into potting soils.

Sometimes I put a few rocks in the bottom of pots to help keep top-heavy plants from tipping over, and if a pot is way too big for my plants, I often add empty plastic jugs or other filler material to the bottom to take up space so that the pot needs less potting soil.

infested leaves and spraying with insecticidal soap or misting three or four times with a 50/50 spray of one part alcohol to one part water.

Feeding Landscape Plants: Fertilize for Quality, Not Quantity

There is a lot of emphasis on fertilizing plants, and no doubt they need certain nutrients for good or steady growth and production. But let's face it, many native plants get their nutrients from recycled leaves and wild animal and bird wastes, and lots of plants in abandoned or uncultivated gardens can go for decades without having fertilizers added to their soil—just look around and see for yourself.

And when was the last time Aunt Mary fertilized that old potted philodendron? Two years ago?

Still, there is no doubt that giving cultivated plants an occasional feeding can boost their performance and invigorate them with health-ier leaves, stems, roots, and flowers. But don't be intimidated by people telling you to feed, feed, feed your plants, when the shrillest of them are either fertilizer salesmen (fertilizers are highly profitable for garden centers) or folks intent on winning a blue ribbon (or maybe just brag-ging rights) for the showiest plants.

All plants really need is a little pick-me-up from time to time; overfer-tilizing, either too much at one time or a steady buildup over years, is far worse for most plants than fertilizing too little, or not at all.

What Plants Need

The most important nutrients needed by plants, other than what they get from air and water, are nitrogen, phosphorus, and potassium, followed by calcium and a few others.

In a bag of fertilizer, the amounts of each of the three main nutrients are always listed in a ratio of three numbers (18:6:12, or 13:13:13, or 2:1:1, etc.); these indicate what percentage each of the three makes up of the mix contained in the bag, with the rest being filler. The higher the numbers, the stronger the fertilizer, and the less that is needed to feed plants.

In other words, though there are important "side" benefits from using manures and other natural fertilizers, they are generally lower in nutri-ents than synthetic fertilizers, meaning it takes more to supply the same nutrients as synthetic kinds with higher numbers on the bag. Conversely, it is easier to overfertilize or even damage plants using highly concen-trated synthetic fertilizers (though even organic nitrogen fertilizers can burn plants when overused).

Note: Few gardeners have their soil tested for nutrient deficiencies; however, it is good to have a soil test done every few years as a "bench-mark" to see if you are using enough or too much, and to see if your soil pH can be adjusted a little to help fertilizers work better.

In a nutshell, this is a brief summary of how these nutrients help plants grow best:

Nitrogen (N, the first number in the ratio on the bag) literally makes plants grow stems and leaves, but generally it does not last very long in most soils. Foliage plants (lawn, ferns, lettuce) like a little extra nitrogen, but too much at a time often forces green growth at the expense of flow-ers or fruit (all vine, no tomatoes) or causes plants to grow too quickly, making them weak and tender, or even "burning" or killing them. Use nitrogen fertilizers once or twice a year, lightly. Whenever possible, use a natural ("organic") source of nitrogen, or at least a "slow-release" form of synthetic nitrogen—but as always, be careful never to overuse fertilizers, even natural forms, or you risk plant damage.

Phosphorus (P, the second number) doesn't "make" flowers and fruit the way nitrogen makes plants grow (whether they want to or not), but it does help them produce better-quality flowers and fruits. Too much phosphorus, applied too frequently, though, can interfere with other nutrients, especially nitrogen. Once phosphorus levels in your soil are adequate (as indicated by a soil test), adding phosphorus once every year or two is usually plenty.

Potassium or potash (K, the third number) helps plant stems and roots grow stronger and lowers a plant's freezing point (it's the so-called winterizer ingredient in lawn fertilizers). Though not as soluble as nitrogen, it washes away easily in sandy soils and should be applied every two or three years. This is often the most difficult nutrient to find in ready-to-use natural or organic forms, though there are mineral sources such as greensand that will help raise potassium levels in the soil over time. Seaweed fertilizers also often have higher amounts of potassium.

Calcium (Ca) helps plants in many ways, including preventing "blossom end rot" of tomatoes and peppers. It is available in agricultural lime and should be added every few years if a soil test indicates a deficiency. By the way, eggshells in the compost add calcium to the soil as well.

Micronutrients, sometimes called "trace elements," are needed in very small amounts for overall plant health, growth, and production. They include iron, zinc, boron, and a few others. They are some-

Plain dirt can grow great gardens but needs feeding with fertilizers.

Growing healthy plants starts with healthy soil. Period.

what available in most garden soils, especially clay soils; however, poor or sandy soils, and potting soils, generally require them to be added.

Though these minerals are available separately (adding tiny amounts of household materials such as Epsom salts, boric acid, or even paper matches—the heads of which contain magnesium—can provide certain micronutrients), it is best to use a rich compost or a good-quality fertilizer that has these minerals listed on the label.

Types of Fertilizers

Fertilizers can be found in many forms: loose, as in manures or compost; as dry granules to be added to the soil; in water-soluble forms to be mixed with water and poured around roots or onto plants; or as specialty "slow-release" beads to be used in potting soils.

In general, liquid fertilizers, being water-soluble, are quickly washed out of soils and require more frequent application than slow-to-dissolve granules.

By the way, compost tea can be made by steeping fresh compost for a few days in water, with occasional aeration; it is then poured around and onto plants. It is a suitable fertilizer with proven antifungal properties.

Although specialty plant fertilizers can be found for nearly any kind of plant (vegetables, roses, African violets, bulbs) and are perfectly fine if not used too strongly or too often, they are expensive and usually unnecessary. Synthetic ("chemical") fertilizers, though inexpensive and fast-acting, are easily overdone and can harm worms and other soil organisms, as well as wash away into waterways and cause problems downstream.

Plus, synthetic fertilizers do not "feed" the soil or its organisms—an all-important consideration for those gardeners who understand the crucial link between healthy soil and healthy plants.

For these reasons, most "whole-garden" experts (this author included) prefer to use—at least mostly—natural fertilizers, including compost, manure, and other natural sources of plant nutrients.

The takeaway message is this: just don't ever overdo it with fertilizers. "Lean and mean" is the best way to keep plants growing but still tough.

Tools and Equipment

There are tools, and there are tools. Like good cooks, most gardeners have favorite tools they use over and over, all the time, and other tools that simply gather dust in the garage or take up space in the toolshed. Still others are used rarely but are irreplaceable labor-savers when they do get pulled out and put to use.

For most gardeners, certain big items are too useful to do without: mowers, leaf blowers, string trimmers, leaf shredders, and lawn edgers come to mind. But though these gas-powered tools (and their more limited but energy-efficient electric cousins) are certainly good to have when needed, many gardeners find they can get by without them, or rent or borrow what they need only occasionally. Or hire out the job in the first place.

My personal opinion is, if it's too big a job to do, why do it at all? Is there an easier approach you could take? Could the garden be redesigned by choosing a different style (naturalistic tree-form shrubs versus tightly pruned gumdrop-shaped shrubs)? Could the lawn be made smaller, surrounded with more environment- and gardener-friendly plants?

Quintessential Garden Tools

Quintessence refers to the medieval philosophy that a fifth element— after earth, air, fire, and water—was what heavenly bodies and other unexplained objects were made of. Nowadays it refers to objects that represent the very essence of simplicity or of purpose. In most cases they are used for only one thing, but they do it so well they cannot be replaced with anything as perfectly apt.

If some of these objects did not exist, someone would quickly invent them. Think computer mouse, tea bags, and that strainer thing in the sink.

Now apply it to the garden. When my horticulturist great-grandmother passed away, I made sure that I would end up with her dozens of antique "flower frogs"—variously shaped metal, ceramic, or glass weights with holes or pins in them for holding flowers upright in vases. They only do one thing, and nothing can beat them (except maybe those green water-absorbing foam blocks that florists use, but that are only used once and discarded).

Long before humans started wearing shoes—or gloves, for that matter—they figured out that a sharp stick was better than a finger for poking holes in the ground for seeds. So the "dibble" was invented, and today you can buy neatly tapered ones with metal tips and even T handles for a better grip.

Other quintessential tools that I simply cannot garden well with-out include a flat-bladed border spade, used to turn soil over for new beds and keep edges neat; a regular shovel with its scoop for moving piles of stuff into or out of my wheelbarrow; a sturdy digging fork with which I mix compost into soil, fluff up soil between plants, and turn my compost; and hand prun-ers and lopping shears for keeping fruit trees, roses, and other plants in line.

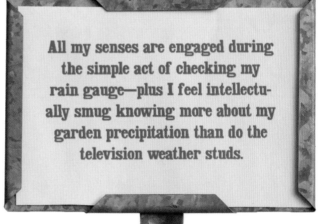

All my senses are engaged during the simple act of checking my rain gauge—plus I feel intellectu-ally smug knowing more about my garden precipitation than do the television weather studs.

Because I have containers and hang-ing baskets, I love my garden hose—or, better yet, the little valve on the end of my garden hose that helps me turn the water on, off or down to a trickle from my end instead of having to walk all the way back to the faucet. Best step-saver since text messaging.

I am often gone from my garden for days or weeks at a time, including in the hot summer; because I'm no Luddite, I use drip irrigation on my container plants. The best part is the simple timer I use to have the water come on and shut off every two or three days while I am gone (see Drip Irrigation sidebar on page 126).

When I'm home, I depend on my rain gauge for helping me feel superior to the weather guys on TV, who at best can only guess at how much precipitation my garden actually gets. Every time I go out to check it, I am engaged physically with all my senses: the sights and sounds of the garden; the feel of temperature on my skin (and the unexpected way my feet can feel—right through my shoes—the difference between my deck, my walkway, and the garden mulch as I walk to and from the rain gauge); the flavors of berries I pick as I pass them; and the sharply sweet bouquet of rosemary as I brush through it along the walk.

And how could I get by without my collection of five-gallon buckets with their sturdy handles? I use them constantly for hauling all sorts of stuff, mixing potting soil, harvesting vegetables, and maybe throwing over a surprised garden snake.

As far as uncomplicated tools go, nothing can beat an old-fashioned, flat-bladed, metal "bastard" file for keeping shovels, spades, and hoes sharp. But to make it even more perfect, how about that wooden handle that screws onto the end of the file, for a better grip?

Though I don't own a lawn mower (my personal garden has no turfgrass at all—call me lazy, but I'd rather spread brown mulch a couple of times a year than mow green grass every couple of weeks), I do enjoy occasionally using my gas-powered string trimmer to knock down spent wildflowers and edge my beds. And though I enjoy the feel and sound—and exercise—of my sturdy leaf rake and deck broom, on rare occasions a powerful leaf blower really comes in handy for quickly corralling leaf litter after a big windstorm or right before garden guests arrive.

Simple tools need no instructions.

There are other simple tools and equipment most gardeners can't perform without: a ladder, sturdy boots, string and wire, waterproof marking pens, and a small stick for moving stuff (including spider webs) out of the way. They all have three things in common:

they are useful, they are enjoyable, and, for most of them, I am their only moving part.

In a word, they are *quintessential.*

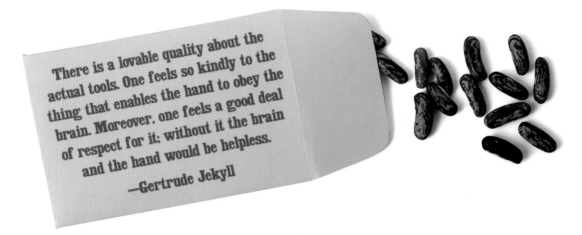

There is a lovable quality about the actual tools. One feels so kindly to the thing that enables the hand to obey the brain. Moreover, one feels a good deal of respect for it; without it the brain and the hand would be helpless.

—Gertrude Jekyll

Pruning

Whacking on plants with implements of destruction is more than just a fun way to vent one's frustrations—it is an important act of gardening, without which we would soon be wrapped up in vines dripping from low-hanging limbs and pushed off our walkways by spreading plant thugs.

There are well-meaning but misguided gardeners who have been taught that certain forms of pruning constitute crimes against nature (see the sidebar following this section). To them I say, "Then just don't do it."

Truth is, there are important reasons for pruning trees, shrubs, and some perennials. Many landscape shrubs and vines are clipped regularly for size control, shaping, and neatness and to keep them from crowding one another, obstructing views or walks, or tangling in your hair.

In general, with the exception of hedges and small shrubs, thinning wayward branches is preferred over shearing, which thickens growth but usually requires regular repetition.

The best rules of thumb for when to prune really involve *when not* to prune: wait until spring bloomers finish flowering before pruning, and avoid pruning anything within a couple of months of winter, to allow new growth time to come out and "harden off" before freezing weather arrives.

Pruning fruit trees and vines is almost a necessity, to help keep the plants vigorous, to reduce limb breakage under heavy fruit loads, to open the plants up for better air circulation (to reduce conditions that encourage diseases), and to make harvesting easier. This kind of pruning is usually done in the winter, when plants are fully dormant, but varies from fruit to fruit. For more information, consult any university extension office or any book or online source that deals with fruit production.

Climbing roses, like vines, are simply thinned to remove errant or cluttered canes.

Other reasons for pruning include removing injured, broken, diseased, or dead plant parts (which can be done any time of the year) and "rejuvenating" overgrown shrubs—cutting them back nearly to the ground to stimulate strong, healthy new growth. This should not be done to "needle-leaf" plants (conifers such as junipers, yew, pines, arborvitae, etc.), which cannot recover from such hard pruning.

Some plants require regular pruning to be productive.

Pests: Bugs, Blights, and Weeds

> *Bugs are not going to inherit the earth—they already own it . . . we might as well make peace with the landlord.*
> —Thomas Eisner

For better or worse, things that go "bump" in the garden are simply part of gardening, and some of them make their way indoors from time to time. If not for them, Eden would be on every corner—and even then,

FALSE ARREST FOR CRAPE MURDER

A lot of horticulturists have been teaching gardeners that pruning crape myrtles and other multistemmed trees and shrubs into sticks with wooden balls at the ends is a bad thing. I suggest that they are being hypocritical—or, at best, disingenuous.

This practice, called *pollarding*, has been done for centuries as a way to keep tall plants low (mostly for reaching fruit) and to provide a ready source of material for weaving into "wattle" fences. An extreme form called *coppicing* is used to cut multi-trunk trees nearly to the ground every three or four years to provide uniform fence posts.

Neither practice seriously harms the trees, any more than cutting roses hard every winter harms the shrubs.

In fact, it is no more unnatural than clipping poodles (originally done to help the game dogs swim better while protecting their vital organs from cold), or plucking errant eyebrows.

Pollarding is not bad, it is just pollarding. To say otherwise is to impose personal taste onto others—which is a social concern, not a horticultural one.

To those who cry foul when someone pollards a plant, I say *back off*.

Pollarding has been used for centuries to provide small twigs for garden use.

some of the most beloved plants on Earth, including fantastic native wildflowers and seedlings from wonderful shade trees, could become noxious weeds in the garden. And it often seems as if the most beautiful butterflies lay eggs that hatch into the most voracious caterpillars.

In my garden, I always leave a few of the striped caterpillars eating my parsley and fennel, and a handful of giant tomato hornworms, knowing they will turn into giant swallowtail butterflies and the huge "hawk"

Fantastic forms can be created through topiary.

LET SOME PLANTS AND HEDGES GROW INFORMALLY

Instead of keeping everything tightly sheared—which is an interesting Slow Gardening hobby in itself called *topiary* (watch out for wasp nests in the summer!)—consider letting some grow up into small trees. You may end up with more flowers and berries, plus bird nesting, with less effort.

To do this, simply thin out the lower limbs as they grow taller, and remove a few branches from those you leave, to create a more naturalistic effect. If a plant gets too large for its space, consider removing it and replacing it with something more appropriate.

I know this is troublesome, at least at first. But again, Slow Gardeners take a long view of things, and this can be an interesting new approach, at least with a few normally sheared plants.

moths that come out at dusk to pollinate my evening four o'clocks and moonvines.

Truth is, gardens naturally attract wildlife—and not just pretty birds and butterflies. Often they are filled with critters—some beneficial, some not so nice.

For starters, there are bees and wasps; spiders, scorpions, and centipedes; snakes, lizards, frogs, and toads; snails and slugs; fire ants and fireflies; nematodes, earthworms, and caterpillars; crows and mockingbirds; stinkbugs, crickets, giant mutant grasshoppers, whiteflies, and aphid/greenflies; and pocket gophers, squirrels, moles, voles, rats, rabbits, armadillos, chipmunks, skunks, and woodchucks—oh, and deer. And sometimes, unruly neighborhood kids. Where does the list end?

A variety of bizarre but harmless creatures can be found in gardens.

What to Do

Some pests (including weeds) we simply don't understand, or they are more nuisance than pest; quite a few insects actually feed on flower nectar like bees, and the larvae of some are beneficial as they eat and decompose fallen leaves and other organic debris. Some weeds are actually good "living mulches" for larger plants.

A couple of generations ago all we could do with destructive pests was to "go with the flow"—plant enough for everyone, including the pests, and replant as needed.

Then, in just the last half century, we got into a race to find ever-more-potent chemical solutions, a pie-in-the-sky "shotgun" approach that often caused more problems than it solved. Now most of the "good ones" are gone, victims of their own potency or overuse.

Nowadays, the term "pest control" no longer means total eradication, it means "abatement"—knocking down the worst, and living with a certain amount of pest damage. And a safer, more moderate approach is emerging, called "integrated pest management" or IPM. It simply involves using several different practices rather than expecting a magic wand to save us at the last minute.

Besides, owing to many common chemicals being taken off the market in recent years for environmental or health reasons, there are some very effective "natural" alternatives—like microbial controls for certain insects, and concentrated plant oils for weed control—that have been around awhile but are now getting less expensive because of supply and demand.

Pesticide Use

In many cases—especially when the choice is between having an important plant or losing it entirely—some pesticides, either natural or synthetic, can be used with little or no harm to nearby other plants, critters, the environment, or your health. But for the best, and safest, results, *you must learn a little first.*

Learn what your specific pest is, choose something labeled for that pest, use it exactly according to directions, repeat as needed, and follow all sorts of precautions, from waiting a certain period after application to harvest a vegetable to being very careful about disposing of the container.

Not sure what to do? Don't depend on what you read on the Internet, unless it's from a reliable source, and don't automatically take the word of someone who sells pesticides for a living. Contact your county extension service for good advice—and ask about natural controls when you do—before spending a lot of money on useless or dangerous "snake oil" remedies sold to frustrated gardeners.

After all that, if reasonable efforts at using pesticides don't work, it may be best to simply

Soft insects including aphids (greenflies) can be controlled with safe sprays containing natural soaps.

dump the plant or rework the flower bed, and replace the problem plants with something less stressful.

It's not as if plants are like an aging pet dog or something; when you are faced with a "do something or lose your plants" situation, simply decide whether or not the plant is worth the cost and the effort—and the anxiety—of selecting, buying, and using a pesticide, then select the safest, least harmful control, and don't overdo it.

Diseases

Spotted leaves, spoiled fruit, patchy lawns, rotten roots, hollowed-out stems, dead twigs, mushy tomatoes: these are just a few of the common

DEUS EX MACHINA

Anyone remember the old *Twilight Zone* program in which aliens come to Earth with all sorts of human-helping powers and world-saving abilities, but in the end their *How to Serve Man* manual is outed as a cookbook? Such miraculous bailouts often turn into not-so-benign horror stories.

It's the same with gardening. Whenever a new, seemingly spontaneous "cure" comes along for fire ants, lawn stickers, or voracious garden-eating critters, a subtle but high price seems to come with it.

Reminds me of the deus ex machina, or the "god from a machine," that old stage device used in Greek and Roman dramas in which an apparently insoluble crisis is solved at the last minute by the intervention of a "god," usually descending onstage by a wire suspended from a crane or some other elaborate piece of equipment. It's the

"saved by the cavalry" thing you might see in old Western pictures.

Anyway, I've been thinking about this "pie in the sky" approach to gardening. It took us a couple of generations to catch on to the fact that almost every newfangled pest-eradicating chemical caused terrible, unforeseen hits on "non-target" species of plants, birds, or other wildlife and sometimes ruined drinking water supplies. And the pests still managed to outmaneuver (or out-evolve) the chemical treatment, only to come back with vengence.

Truth is, gardening is a constant bailing of a very leaky boat. When last-minute scientific breakthroughs fail, we should continue to either work harder at tried-and-true remedies or garden smarter by doing less counterintuitive stuff like planting high-maintenance or pest-predictable plants.

ways diseases affect our gardens. And they can be terribly destructive. Some are nearly impossible to avoid.

Your best bet for dealing with seriously diseased roses, lawns, vegetables, and other plagued plants is to plant varieties that have been selected or bred to be resistant to the problems, or to plant something else that is nearly as good.

The second-best control is to practice good sanitation: avoid watering late in the day or at night, to reduce the conditions many disease organisms need to spread; make sure plants are well spaced or pruned to allow better air movement to keep foliage dry; avoid overwatering or overfertilizing, which weakens plants; pick up diseased fruit; prune away and remove diseased leaves or other plant parts; and lay down fresh mulch to

"DEER-PROOF" PLANTS

Read my lips: *There are no deer-proof plants.* Oh, I've seen the lists, heard the sworn-to-be-true anecdotes that deer won't eat hellebores or some kinds of hollies and on and on—as if we all want to grow only those few plants. And then there are the desperate applications of various elixirs and soaps, balls of hair, even predator (or gardener) urine.

None of it *really* works, for everyone. Not for long. Ditto for moles, voles, armadillos, squirrels . . . Roger Swain, who wrote the foreword to this book, put up such a high, heavy deer fence around his New Hampshire garden, it reminded me of the Tyrannosaurus fencing in the movie *Jurassic Park*. He put it up because he thought it was necessary, in spite of the expense and effort, to preserve his garden. And it works.

At times, this strategy pretty much goes for insects as well. (I'm thinking especially of flea beetles, cabbage moths, and their green caterpillar larvae.) About the only solution is a physical barrier such as "floating row covers" (lightweight fabric) to cover plants—it's the insect equivalent of the high-tensile deer fence.

Bottom line: fencing—tall metal fences, double-strand electric fences, lightweight but surprisingly strong (and nearly invisible) plastic deer netting—is the only dependable deer deterrent. Period.

Anyone saying otherwise, please tell those of us who maintain public parks and botanical gardens for a living. We'd love to find something more suitable than the scheduling of discreet, off-hour archery sessions.

reduce the spread of spores. Also, plant early enough in the season to get a good harvest before diseases get too bad, and replant if needed to have healthy new plants coming along as replacements.

Note: Fungicides—natural or not—do not cure diseases; they merely provide a protective film over new or otherwise unprotected plant parts. Because they wear off, wash off, or break down in sunlight, usually within days or a week or two, they need to be reapplied regularly when disease conditions are present. Use a fungicide or other suppressing spray to prevent disease organisms from spreading and causing further damage, not to try to "cure" the disease.

And keep in mind the unpleasant fact that, with some plant diseases, it may be easiest in the long run to simply plant something else.

Plant diseases mar the beauty of some plants.

Tips for Reducing or Dealing with Pests

What can you do when problems raise their sometimes thorny heads?

First, a simple truth: if your shrubs or flowers have little bugs or blots or spots or raggedy edges, try looking at them from ten feet away. Take off your glasses, stop obsessing, and a lot of garden "headaches" disappear. Even some weeds can be seen as "ground covers" that complement the colors and textures of your other plants. Really.

Some weeds can be pulled, chopped, or mulched out of existence; others will inexorably take over the tidiest garden. Damaging insects can be thumped, picked, trapped, or eaten by beneficial critters; many, though, will destroy entire plants. Plants with severe diseases—fungal, bacterial, viral, and even stress-related environmental ones—may shed leaves, have flowers ruined or roots rotted, or worse, just look bad; pruning or replanting is often the only resort.

But if your garden is really suffering beyond what you can live with, and you positively identify that it is a pest doing the damage—bug, disease, or weed—then you need to make a big decision about whether it's worth doing anything about.

What you can't see may not be much of a problem to your plants; a lot of plant problems can safely be ignored. If that's not possible, though, here are some other easy tips for avoiding pesticide use:

- Avoid growing plants that have predictably serious pests, or look for pest-resistant varieties.
- Mix up your plantings—especially flowers and vegetables— and make sure related plants are separated by non-related plants, so pests don't have a field day moving down a row

SNAKES IN THE GARDEN

Like it or not, unless you live in England (or Ireland, where Saint Patrick drove them out), the occasional snake is part of the landscape. The vast majority of snakes are harmless—unless you try to pick one up, which is very unlikely to ever, ever happen. Most snakes are good for the garden; they, along with lizards, toads, and frogs, are biologically beneficial and keep bugs in check, and none of them have enough brains to be aggressive. Here's some good advice: learn to turn stuff (rocks, old boards, brush piles) over carefully, and be prepared to jump back, then calm down and move on.

Harmless, nonpoisonous snakes patrol many a garden unseen.

of similar plants. Move them around every year to reduce pest buildup.

- Keep plants healthy with good soil, mulch, deep and infrequent watering, and light fertilization so they will fend off or recover quickly from pest attacks.

- Hand-pull as many weeds as you can, keeping on top of them to prevent them from getting too large and difficult to pull, and before they set seed to spread even worse. Mulches help greatly with weed-seed suppression. If you must use a weeding tool, keep it sharp for ease and effective use.

- Introduce or encourage beneficial insects in your garden, and learn to live with some bad bugs (without aphids, ladybugs would starve).

Beneficial insects help keep many insects in check.

- Perfection is unobtainable; lighten up on minor or cosmetic imperfections.

- Try "mechanical" controls (handpicking big pests, pruning out infested plant parts) instead of spraying pesticides, even "natural" ones.

- Include a few plants and a water feature to attract insect-eating birds into the garden, or even "insectary" plants such as members of the carrot, mint, and onion families, to attract the kinds of bugs that eat other bugs.

- Many pesticides—including the "natural" ones (elemental, botanical, or biological)—can be toxic in certain concentrations to people, pets, beneficial insects, fish, or other forms of wildlife aside from the targeted insect pests. If you must use any pesticide in the garden, be sure to consult several sources, and choose the one that will do the job without endangering your health, your garden, or your environment. Always use it exactly according to the instructions and precautions on the label. And bear in mind that, just like aspirin (a naturally derived medicine), any pesticide can be overused.

• Try not to get dependent on any one pest-control method, which pests eventually find a way around anyway.

These guidelines are nothing new—just good gardening practices used by gardeners for many centuries. They're still worth following—maybe more now than ever.

Weeds

A weed is any plant having to deal with an unhappy human.
— J. C. Raulston

Unwanted plants have a tendency to crop up in the best gardens. They overcrowd, smother, or shade out our "good" plants, harbor insects and other vermin, rob our prized plants of nutrients and water, and upset our muse.

Sometimes the worst weeds are actually valuable plants—in someone else's garden. It is ironic how the North American native wildflower called fireweed has taken over much of England's countryside (where it is called rosebay willow-herb), and Europe's purple loosestrife has taken over North America's wetlands—and yet, at a glance, to most gardeners they look almost exactly alike. But each in its way is causing problems in the other's native land.

Weeds come in all shapes, sizes, and plant types. Some can be pulled or chopped out of existence (this takes diligence and patience), some can be smothered with mulches, and some can be shaded out by taller plants. Some you may simply have to live with.

As is the garden such is the gardener. A man's nature runs either to herbs or weeds. —Francis Bacon

Most gardens require weed control.

But what is a weed, if not a plant growing where you don't want it? Is it possible to live with some, or is the ideal of a perfect mono-crop lawn or neatly mulched flower bed too embedded in our minds to resist? Can't moss, which grows quite naturally in shaded, compacted acidic soil, be a good substitute for a lawn that is struggling or dying in the same conditions?

My mother—a respectable gardener in her own right, maintaining her own horticulturist grandmother's estate garden—found the best solution of all: "Whenever I find a weed I simply cannot get rid of, I just plant something taller or weedier than it, and let 'em fight it out on their own."

By the way, there are saving graces to some weeds. In the vegetable garden, they can be efficient "dynamic accumulators" (tapping nutrients from the soil) and can make good mulch around crop plants—or good ingredients for the compost pile. And it also pays to identify even the worst weeds, to see how other gardeners learn to simply contain them, or even use them.

Some weeds are even perfectly edible—dandelions, chickweed, lamb's-quarters, bamboo, even kudzu in the South. In other words, as with the destructive European brown snail in California, which is what

DEALING WITH PLANT DEATH

Sooner or later, there comes a time to say goodbye to a cherished shrub, potted plant, or entire garden bed. It may be due to season-ending weather (who hasn't been sad when a lush summer garden is killed by frost?), disease, lightning, or just old age, but a garden is filled with as much death as it is life.

Dead and dying plants are just part of gardening, as is thinning vegetables that have been planted too thickly. You simply can't save them all! This is what compost piles are for—recycling plants so they have a better life in the next crop.

Even ancient historic plants die, sometimes taking decades to slowly fall apart. The best way to handle this is to plant something fresh that may someday *become* historic.

Better yet, learn to propagate great plants by means of seeds, cuttings, or grafting, so you can at least have a piece of the original to carry on, preserve, and share with other gardeners.

they call *escargot* in France, *if you can't beat 'em, eat 'em*—which is a lot more satisfying than spraying them!

Plant Propagation: Share the Wealth

Separating a clump of plants is the only time you can divide and multiply at the same time.
   —anonymous
Sharing plants is like love—the more you give, the more you get.
   —anonymous

Gardeners have always been a sharing lot; most of us cling to a favorite plant, or at least its memory, from when we were first gifted with it from someone else's garden. Luckily, many cherished plants are downright easy to propagate; otherwise they would never have been shared in the first place.

Multiply, spread, and share your own plants by saving seed, digging and dividing in-ground parts of multiple-stemmed perennials and shrubs, or rooting pieces of stems.

These techniques and more (layering, grafting, bulb scaling, even laboratory tissue culture) are well covered in nearly all general gardening books and magazines, and much more detail is available online for specific plants.

In general, seeds should be collected from mature seedpods or from mature fruits (including those enormous yellow cucumbers and other crops that are left out way past the eating stage). Some can be stored for a year or more if kept in a cool, dry place; others need to be sown immediately. Sometimes a special treatment is needed to get the seeds out of the fruit or seedpod, like fermenting tomato seeds or washing magnolia and dogwood seed to remove the gelatinous, germination-inhibiting seed coat.

Though some herbaceous perennials that grow in clumps, such as daylilies, irises, and bulbs, can be dug and divided nearly any time of the year, the best time is usually when they are dormant, or at least in the season opposite of when they flower the most. Replant the divisions immediately, or keep them moist and in a lightly shaded area until you can get them back in the ground.

Woody shrubs and vines that grow in multistemmed clumps or send up "suckers" from underground stems, such as raspberry, spirea, ivy, and wisteria, are best separated and moved while fully dormant, usually in late fall or winter.

Cuttings taken from evergreen shrubs—azaleas, hollies, boxwood, and the like—are best taken in early to midsummer, from sturdy, semi-mature new shoots, and rooted in light shade and high humidity; consider making a small clear "tent" from plastic sheeting, or at least covering the cuttings with clear plastic bottles with the bottoms cut off and the bottle caps removed to prevent the buildup of steamy heat inside. Cuttings taken from deciduous plants such as roses, crape myrtle, althaea (rose of Sharon), and similar plants that drop their leaves in the winter are best rooted in the late fall or winter and left in place over the first season to get well rooted before being planted out in their permanent spots.

The use of rooting hormones can increase the number of cuttings that root successfully, but this is not necessary if you just make a few more cuttings to offset any possible losses. (Your grandmother probably didn't use any rooting hormones—she just stuck cuttings in the ground in the right season.)

While there are plenty of how-to books and online sites for more specific propagation techniques, here are some very general guidelines that will get most gardeners by without a lot of detail:

- Root deciduous shrubs in the fall or late winter; root evergreens in the summer.
- Divide perennials in the season opposite of when they bloom.
- Save mature (ripened) seed early in the season to avoid pest buildup and as insurance against a bad season.
- Collect and propagate seed from native plants and wildflowers rather than removing the plants themselves from the wild.
- Grow enough to share with others.
- When sowing seed, keep in mind how long it takes for the plant to mature, flower, and set more seed, making sure the plants have enough time to mature before your area's seasonal bad weather typically sets in.

Heirloom plants grown from seed are typically "open pollinated"—their seeds come true year after year, as opposed to hybrids, whose seeds often do not.

Gardening in Tune with Yourself

There are countless sources of more detailed information on all aspects of growing plants, but gardening is about doing things, from choosing adapted plants and materials to doing all the little chores required to keep plants growing well.

With minor variations for climate, soil, and garden style, most basic horticultural practices are used—for better or worse—by all gardeners, from accomplished gardeners with specific goals in mind to folks who love just puttering around.

You don't have to feel like a cult member to see how the following ideas can save you time, money, and effort in the garden, while actually helping your garden look and work better—and increasing your gardening enjoyment.

In fact, they *could* be seen as effort-saving and frugal (lazy and cheapskate) approaches. No matter what your motivation, as a bonus, they happen to help you and your family, the environment in your neighborhood, the country, and the world—all at the same time.

Take a quick look at the following quick tips, and ponder their use in your garden.

- Redesign the lawn to be smaller and more sensible.
- Choose drought-hardy pest-resistant native or adapted nonnative plants.

- Plant more trees and shrubs, in groups and masses.
- Plant shade vines on an arbor over the patio and on west-facing walls.
- Use natural slow-release fertilizers to feed the soil as well as your plants.
- Mulch to conserve water and help control weeds.
- Control weeds and insect pests naturally, through physical or biological—not chemical—solutions.
- Add plants that attract butterflies and bees; put up a bat house.
- Lose the leaf blower and leaf shredder—use "human-powered" tools.
- Grow some of your own vegetables, fruits, and culinary herbs.
- Make compost—or at least have a leaf pile.
- Collect and use rain water.
- Create a "rain garden" sump.
- Install low-voltage or even solar-powered night lighting.
- Use drip irrigation as much as possible.
- Put the water garden pump on a timer.
- Reject perfection—Nature is not perfect, and you don't have to be, either.

The main thing is, first, to understand the basics, and then to explore all the possibilities as you find your own level of challenge or comfort. Do the best you can, and enjoy what you do.

And embrace change. Above all, Slow Gardening is not a static list of "how-to" garden rules.

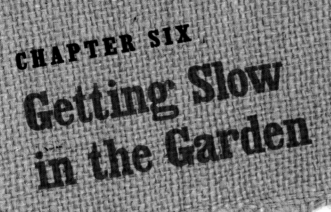

CHAPTER SIX
Getting Slow in the Garden

The Slow Gardening concept is very inclusive, with plenty of room for many different approaches that will work just fine for nearly anyone—make that *everyone*—regardless of personality or interests. Whatever your bliss, it is yours to discover and follow.

That said, here are a few easy examples of ways in which many people find garden-related outlets for their muses, their curiosity, even their frustrations—ways in which gardeners slow down and focus on the here and now, to savor their lives through everyday practices.

Keep in mind that it's natural for a lot of people, particularly for gifted left-brained types who are naturally bent on categorizing and organizing everything (including the people around them), to try and make sense out of simple concepts by coming up with lots of guidelines and rules.

But, as has been mentioned over and over in this book, Slow Gardening is an attitude, not a checklist of things to do—or not do.

This chapter highlights a few of the many, many ways people are slowing down to create a garden lifestyle that gives them extra pleasure. It is by no means all-encompassing, but it does offer some starting points for consideration. Each of the following concepts could easily fill its own entire book (most, in fact, have), yet for every one of them, there are many more not addressed.

All good work is done the way ants do things: Little by little.
—Lafcadio Hearn

First Things First: Stop Planting Like a Farmer

Gardening is rarely a race.

Certainly, people who make their living growing plants, including farmers, fruit and vegetable producers, and horticulturists who run plant nurseries, have to take weather and market trends into consideration and plan ahead carefully to make sure they plant in time for a timely harvest later on. Seasons are important to them.

And gardeners with large-space or long-term vegetable crops such as corn, peas, potatoes, or melons may need to till up a lot of soil at one time and plant according to the season, which often requires tillers and other power equipment. While this sort of system may be easier or even necessary in large gardens, which are usually managed more efficiently in big rushes, truth is, this kind of gardening is really just small-scale farming.

But most home gardeners—especially those with small garden plots, flower beds, raised beds, and container gardens—simply plant stuff whenever they feel like it, just about any time; then, when it's ready to be harvested or at its season's end, they simply pull up the old plants, rework the soil, and sooner or later get around to planting something else in the same space.

This cycle of doing what you want, a bit at a time, when you get around to it, has many advantages, including keeping a little something coming and going throughout the entire growing season. This kind of system makes the most efficient use of space and takes less time and effort to get the chore done. Plus you minimize the sense of dread or guilt about something that you always "should be doing." Life is too short to worry about the garden: the whole point is to make gardening a pleasure, not turn it into a burden or a part-time job.

Spread Out Your Chores

Weekends, especially in the spring, are precious time, helping us to renew our spirits and recharge our batteries. The best strategy in the garden, or with any household tasks, is to do a little as you go, instead of loading up all your free days with work and half-killing yourself in the spring.

The old proverb goes "It is better to weed twice, than once," meaning if you wait until the weeds are large, they will be harder to get out of the garden than if you just pull a few every time you notice them.

Some farm practices are satisfying, but following traditional planting seasons doesn't always apply to year-round gardening.

To keep garden chores from building up, every morning as I wander down my garden path to the street to pick up the newspaper, I make a point of setting down my cup of coffee to dawdle along the path and do a little something. Whether it's snipping off errant branches in my face, pulling a few weeds (which, because I pick them while young and before they go to seed, I throw over behind the bushes), or watering a few potted plants, I manage to get a lot done in a little time each day.

Because a lot of these little things get done all along, when the weekend comes I have plenty of time to visit friends, hit the farmers' market, watch a ball game, take my dog camping, and just generally goof off.

Instead of wringing my hands over having too much to do when the weather is nicest and other activities beckon, I try to lighten up on what needs to be done all at once by being a little proactive. I plan ahead and do chores before I'm up against a drop-dead last-minute deadline—knowing there will always be something else I would much rather be doing.

HARD-WIRED FOR EXCITEMENT

Per aspera ad astra (through difficulties to the stars).

Ever wonder why we are so easily lured into buying unfamiliar new plants, tools, or products? Scientists have identified a primitive area of the brain that makes us adventurous.

It's like jumping out of an airplane with a parachute—an act that requires either supreme faith or chutzpah, at least the first time out. The nerve to jump comes from convincing ourselves that we will actually survive the experience, and even enjoy it—thus overcoming our innate fear.

British researchers using brain scans to measure blood flow discovered that a region of the brain known as the *ventral striatum*, which helps process rewards in the brain through the release of "feel good" substances, is more active when people choose unusual objects or do unorthodox things. The scientists think

that this indicates an evolutionary advantage in trying new things and taking simple risks—as long as we think they may prove advantageous in the long run.

Apparently our minds have certain tricks that help us derive pleasure in unexpected places. Pleasure is affected by what a person thinks about the activity—and only we can decide if what we are doing is pleasant. And that often depends on whether we can convince ourselves that it is a good thing to do—whatever that takes.

In other words, humans have the ability to enjoy doing something that is inherently not enjoyable, such as eating hot peppers or mowing a large lawn.

Does this help you reconcile yourself with anything?

Plant Containers

Flowers, herbs, and tropical plants are meant to be enjoyed up close, all year round, indoors as well as on the patio or deck.

By having a few plants growing in pots, we can enjoy gardening every day of the year, even if the weather is too dark, wet, cold, hot, or humid to get very far outside the house. Even in the worst weather, in the worst gardening climate imaginable—perhaps even on spaceships in the future—we can enjoy a tropical paradise indoors, whether that

Small container gardens are interesting mini-paradises.

involves "forcing" flowering bulbs to grow and bloom indoors in gravel and water (see the "Weird Horticultural Trick" sidebar, page 173) or just having a single African violet in bloom on the windowsill. There are many dozens of easy-to-grow plants that tolerate the same temperatures and light found in most homes, apartments, and offices.

Just as an aquarium full of tropical fish can be endlessly entertaining and fascinating, a terrarium can be filled with exotic ferns, cacti, and other plants that otherwise simply can't be grown in your climate. Taking this idea a step further, many gardeners find that keeping pet reptiles, unusual tropical insects (including giant Madagascar "hissing cockroaches"), and tarantula spiders in enclosed terrariums indoors is a fascinating hobby that connects them with nature.

Develop a Long-Term Garden Hobby

There is plenty of room in Slow Gardening for those gardeners who love challenges, pay close attention to detail, and take great pride in their successes. For them, doing something difficult, or doing something well, is a great outlet for their creativity and provides intellectual exercise.

> When your work speaks for itself, don't interrupt.
> — Henry J. Kaiser

Some common gardening hobbies that require focus include amassing and maintaining plant collections (roses, orchids, daffodils, daylilies, hibiscus, cacti, irises, and so on), creating new kinds of plants outright through home hybridizing (of either ornamental or edible plants), making crafts out of homegrown gourds, grafting fruit trees or camellias, pruning small plants into topiaries and bonsai, arranging flowers from homegrown plants, beekeeping, raising fancy chickens, collecting insects, or garden photography.

Getting a "Yard of the Month" award from your own efforts, or even being the first to show up at the neighborhood coffee klatch with ripe homegrown tomatoes, is enough to spur some people into action and put them in touch with their "inner hero."

These and many other hobbies can be all-consuming to some

AMATEUR GARDEN PHOTOGRAPHY

Talk about instant gratification, and easy sharing! The almost overnight advent of "smart" digital cameras, simple computer photo retouching programs, and unlimited sharing opportunities online via e-mail and numerous online photography "communities" has ushered garden photography into a new heyday.

Point-and-click cameras do everything but point themselves and push the button. For most gardeners, a camera should have at least eight or ten "megapixels" for top-quality images and a good closeup lens, and it should shoot well in low light without a flash.

A simple computer program can be used to help get the most out of your efforts. Images can quickly be cropped, lightened, or darkened, have the contrast made more or less sharp, and have the color punched up to be the most realistic. And every image can be "resized" to make it easier to e-mail or download (a major etiquette consideration).

Gardening is too ephemeral not to record; digital cameras make this a snap (pardon the pun).

Outdoor photography has become a major hobby for many gardeners.

people, and just interesting side trips for others. But they are definitely worthwhile pursuits that make them ideal Slow Gardening practices.

The key here is that *you do it yourself*. Don't outsource your pleasure by hiring it out to someone who does it merely for the money.

Garden for All the Senses

The greatest gift of the garden is
the restoration of the five senses.
—Hanna Rion

A garden is an all-senses place, and Slow Gardeners take advantage of as many as they can.

It's easy to garden in ways that stimulate all the senses. I don't want to come across as negative, but it seems as if most folks garden to please others visually. But unless you can smell, feel, taste, and hear your garden as well, it's almost like sensory deprivation.

I have planned my garden so I can open the doors every morning to an easy-to-maintain world that exercises all my senses. Wind chimes are as important as nice fragrances. Fresh homegrown flavors beat mealy-tasting vegetables and fruit trucked in from afar. The goose pimples on my forearm caused by fall's first cold front moving in simply cannot be experienced by watching the late-night weather report. A spider web coated in dew is as amazing to me as a beautiful butterfly. The contrast of golden pine pollen on my green truck makes me smile.

Sight, sound, taste, smell, and touch are the main senses, but there is more to it than that. Everyone has different abilities to gather in these stimuli, and we all have vastly different responses—or reactions—to them.

And still there are other senses, including a sense of place—the *terroir* mentioned

Don't be a couch potato: use the great senses you've been given.

WEIRD HORTICULTURAL TRICK

Talk about doing something just for the interest of it! Nearly every year, late in the fall, I put a handful of fragrant "paperwhite" bulbs (*Narcissus tazetta*) in a bowl of water, prop them up with clean, washed gravel, and add enough water to wet the bottoms of the bulbs. In a few days they sprout roots and green shoots, and within about three weeks they flower.

Along with the midwinter cutting and arranging of stems of early-blooming shrubs like forsythia, quince, and spirea in vases of water, forcing bulbs is one of the fastest ways to bring color and fragrance into midwinter homes. It's an easy activity for bored kids as well as for grownups.

Trouble is, the stems of bulbs grown indoors typically get tall and floppy, and they have to be staked to keep them from falling over under the weight of their flowers. Which brings me to the alcohol trick.

Bill Miller, a horticulture professor and researcher at Cornell University, proved that adding a little distilled alcohol (rubbing alcohol or drinking spirits—not beer or wine) to the bulb water will cause the stems to grow only a third to a half their usual length, though the flowers stay the same full size.

"Too much alcohol is toxic to bulbs; keep it around 5 or 6 percent—using 80-proof liquor (which is 40 percent alcohol), add 1 part liquor to 7 parts water. For rubbing alcohol, which is around 70 percent alcohol, dilute one part with 10 to 11 parts water."

Adding alcohol to water causes forced bulbs to bloom on shorter, sturdier stems.

earlier in this book that makes a garden feel right, and the overall "savory" sensation called *umami*, which is usually associated with taste alone, but which can be extrapolated to mean the overall satisfaction a garden gives, especially when all the senses are employed.

Taste

Once I was prevailed upon to help judge a tomato tasting contest. It was impossible to do, because each of the hundred or so different tomatoes had a unique blend of sweetness and acidity, thickness of its skin and flesh, and even shape and color of the berry itself (botanically speaking, tomatoes are berry fruits).

What made this judging such a farce was that each of the judges had his or her own personal opinion of what makes a tomato taste good in the first place—and no two of them agreed.

So it goes with flavors. I have a personal dislike of slimy things—mouthfeel is a valid reason to reject certain foods—but that's not a taste thing, it's a tactile sensation.

Tastes are detected by buds on our tongues, and they are partly influenced by smell (people who have colds and can't smell find it nearly impossible to tell the difference between an apple and an onion, based on taste alone).

ARE FLOWERS PRETTIER IN ENGLAND?

One of the amazing things I have learned, in my many trips to New England and the Pacific Northwest, and while gardening in Europe, is how a plant can look so good there but seem faded in my own garden in the southeast United States.

It's not that those folks are better gardeners or have cooler plants; it's more *where* they garden. In a nutshell, things just *look* better in these regions, simply because of the angle of the sun.

Just look at how plants appear at midday versus in early morning or late afternoon. When the sun is at a lower angle, blue flowers seem bluer, and greens are more "punched up," simply because of how sunlight passes through more of the atmosphere. Farther south, especially at midday, cooler, more subtle colors like blues and greens appear washed out, and bolder shades like bright reds and yellows tend to dominate. This is why most garden photographers work early and late, and take siestas in the midday.

It's difficult to think anything but pleasant thoughts while eating a homegrown tomato.
—Lewis Grizzard

The main tastes are sweet, sour, bitter, acidic, and savory (*umami*); you could probably throw in the false heat you get from hot peppers as a sixth kind of taste sensation. The main way we use flavor in the garden is when we pick fresh vegetables, fruits, and herbs.

Going beyond tomato contests, an experienced gardener can tell the difference in taste between different varieties of rosemary, peppers, apples, even soil—put a bit of soil to your tongue, and you will find out why old hands called the acidity or alkalinity of their garden soil either "sweet" or "sour."

There is no accounting for taste. But it is one of the main ways we distinguish ourselves from other gardeners.

Sight

Grasses and trees swaying, a garden windmill rotating either lazily or furiously, airborne seeds floating up and down and all around on their way to earth: these are ways you can actually see wind.

We think of sight in the garden as color and texture—and those are certainly important (though not so important as people who design flower beds using color wheels may insist). But sight also gives us clues as to what is going on around us—including motion and heights, slopes, distances, depth perception, and more.

Insects—especially pollinators—approach flowers completely differently than we do, picking up on different wavelengths and patterns to find landing sites near pollen and nectar—patterns we humans can't even see. And many use camouflage to conceal themselves from predators, or to be better predators themselves.

To color-starved people, the bright greens of holly and pine, the softer cedars, and variegated evergreens are more meaningful for their surface texture, which can be discerned even by sight. The slick surface of hollies *looks* smooth, and the furry foliage of garden sage *looks* soft.

A lot of gardeners say there is no color in their gardens, when in fact they are rich with brown hues and shades. True, brown won't be found in a rainbow (it's a mélange of red, yellow, and blue), but though brown is sometimes thought of as a little dull, it's a naturally warm, wholesome color that represents simplicity, friendliness, and dependability.

Back in 1903 when Smith and Binney came out with the first eight-pack Crayola crayon box, brown was there. Over the years they introduced many variations, including raw umber, burnt sienna, taupe, ochre, ecru, and tumbleweed. And who could ever forget the weird one they called *flesh*?

Though I have seen dirt that is nearly black, rusty red, or bluish, it's mostly brown. Dust is light brown, mud is dark brown.

Other hues of brown include auburn, chestnut, cinnamon, russet, tawny, chocolate, tan, brunette, fawn, mahogany, oak, bronze, terracotta, toast, cocoa, coffee, copper, khaki, and beige, And those are just the easy descriptors off the top of my head; a computer search of the color brown, or a visit to any paint store, will boggle your mind.

But what makes them all work so well in the landscape—it's entirely possible to have a good-looking monochromatic winter garden of just browns—is the use of shapes. Think of a medium-brown pine-tree trunk, against the taupe of a dormant winter lawn, with tan pampas grass topped by off-white plumes. Add shredded bark mulch, a wooden bench, a half whiskey barrel planter, and flagstone paving, and there is more than enough to command even the most color-obsessed person's attention.

Anyone with the ability to see beauty never grows old. —Franz Kafka

Brown is a color too.

Plant Blindness

There's a reason why most of us can't see the trees for the forest—we have become "plant blind" from seeing too much at one time, for a long time.

Plant blindness is a fairly new term coined by botanist-educators who have been studying why children are not growing up appreciating plants as much as their grandparents did. Fewer kids have eaten a sun-warmed tomato just picked off the vine, have climbed a tree and felt its bark, or have smelled crushed mint.

This leads to kids not even noticing the plants to begin with—the inability to see or notice the plants in one's environment.

Plant blindness is mostly an eye–brain connection thing; even with our eyes wide open, we simply can't understand all that we see. Think about it this way: What was the color of the last car in front of you at the stoplight? You probably stared right at the license plate, but unless it was highly personalized you didn't "notice" it, right? It's the same with plants, or anything.

Most of us have very efficient sight, with eyes that generate every second some ten million bits of information that are sent to the brain for processing. Trouble is, the brain extracts only about forty bits per second and fully processes a mere sixteen bits that reach our conscious attention. So we react or respond mostly to movement, conspicuous colors, patterns, or other stuff that really stands out. Because plants are all around us all the time and they don't move very much, we see but literally can't process the trees for the forest, unless we make ourselves pay attention. Most of us end up noticing the movement of animals (birds, butterflies, squirrels) rather than the plants themselves, which can easily lead to glossing over the importance of plants. Our brains usually classify most plants—the solar collectors and food- and air-making machines of our planet—as inferior to animals, and plants lose their importance.

We can't see the flowers for the butterflies, and we end up valuing butterflies over the plants they help propagate.

What to do—hug a tree? Better yet, let's give young people the important "little" experiences in touching, smelling, tasting, drawing, and growing plants. Help them to notice, and focus, so they will better understand what is around them.

All life depends on plants. Let's not turn a blind eye to them.

Oh, and throw in some sweetgum balls for extra crunch. I have seen them used on purpose as mulch, and it *looks* quite nice.

Green is great. So is red, yellow, blue, orange, pink, and even gray. But brown is many colors, too. Use them—and textures, motion, and depth perception—to your garden's advantage.

Sound

I can't get from my house to the street without literally brushing through an all-season garden of colorful flowers, tasty herbs and vegetables, and fragrant roses.

And as soon as I open my door I'm awash in pleasant sounds. Most folks, if they stopped to just listen for a minute, would be surprised at the humdrum barrage of urban noise pollution—mostly cars, air conditioners, and lawn mowers. In my garden, these background noises are masked with more soothing sounds.

Sounds are critical to me because of a mild case of tinnitus (ringing in the ears)—no doubt caused by years of listening to loud music and using cheap headphones. Even when I stick my fingers in my ears, I hear a faint but constant high-pitched whine, similar to the singsong of summer cicadas stuck on a high note. I'm not complaining, just justifying; because of this constant whistle, I go to great lengths to put more interesting sounds in my garden.

Some sounds are free, like the mockingbird that interrupts the usual city sounds with its maddening singsong. But I also have placed all sorts of wind chimes around my home— metal, glass, bamboo, even recycled silverware—to create

Wind chimes conjure soothing sounds from thin air.

a soothing cacophony in even the slightest breezes. And at dusk, toads and frogs come out to sing so loudly we can't even hear the interstate or barking dogs.

Both day and night, the sounds from my water gardens take the edge off the city's background noise. An antique iron cauldron in the walled backyard fills the area with its small bubbling fountain. But the front water garden features a small cave above it covered with a large "fall" rock, so water runs over the edge and hits the pond's surface. It faces the front doorway and its splash is aimed and amplified—like when you cup your hands to holler at someone.

From the background "white noise" of my splashy waterfall to the tinkling and bonging of several wind chimes, I have plenty to keep my mind off the ringing in my ears—and the hubbub of the city.

Smell

Humans can detect some ten thousand different odors, which are caused by molecules floating in the air. Our sense of smell is so acute that we can even smell directionally—we can tell just through our noses from which direction a smell originates.

To be overcome by the fragrance of flowers is a delectable form of defeat.
—Beverly Nichols

From enjoying the smell of burning wood in the fire pit to trying to distinguish between the spicy scents of antique roses, we are smelling creatures, yet no two people experience the same exact odor the same way. The sweet fragrance of paperwhite narcissus, one of my all-time favorites, reminded my mother of cat urine.

In my southeastern garden I grow "Mexicali rose," a somewhat invasive perennial *Clerodendrum* with big leaves and large clusters of pink flowers, which has foliage whose smell reminds me of badly spoiled peanut butter. But that's nothing compared with a bizarre "voodoo lily" (*Amorphophallus*) in my back garden. Its nearly four-foot flower, really a spathe (like what you see on caladium), rises from the ground with a thick stem I can barely get my hand around and unfurls a hood that attracts beetles and flies for pollination. Its scent? *Exactly like well-rotted meat.* So strong, it makes visitors check their shoe bottoms.

But when it comes to the "good" fragrances, one thing I had not counted on when I put a solid fence around my garden is how it concentrates fragrances. And sometimes the combinations are enough to make me almost swoon.

It is strong enough in the winter, with narcissus—mostly paperwhites and jonquils—commingling their strong scents with those from the neighborhood's sweet olive, winter honeysuckle shrub, and elaeagnus. Winter fragrances are often elusive, dampened by cool temperatures and dispersed by typically high winds.

But summer is a different story, as the natural chemicals that excite our olfactory senses intensify and waft more slowly in the heavy, humid atmosphere; smells—both good and bad—tend to loll around as if waiting in ambush. Sometimes it is a mélange of roses, ligustrum, honeysuckle, jasmine, and gardenia; each is powerful

Fragrance is perhaps the most memory-inducing, evocative way to share a garden experience.

GOOD SMELL, BAD SMELL

When it comes to good smells/bad smells, what some people relish often gets other people riled up. I personally love heady, sickly-sweet aromas, like lilac and ligustrum, magnolia and gardenia, while some people swear they are allergic to them. However, most fragrant flowers don't cause reactions; usually it is the nearly invisible, wind-blown pollen from trees and grasses that give us sneezing fits.

I should know—some people think I am super-cheerful in the spring and fall, but the truth is, it's the antihistamines, combined with my usual caffeine intake, that make me seem so goofy.

Anyway, a general rule of thumb is that flowers that are pretty or fragrant are "designed" that way to attract pollinating insects, because their pollen is too heavy to blow in the wind and up our noses, to give us headaches and stopped-up sinuses.

enough on its own, but together they often hang over my garden like an invisible fog.

I have even planted "trap" plants—mints and a large rosemary shrub—along my front walk. There is no way anyone can get to my doorstep without brushing past them, making my garden (and my guests) smell like a delightful Mediterranean dish. Some folks balk at this intrusion, but it's an important rite of passage for entering my home.

Touch

As I mentioned earlier, it is impossible to get though my garden without brushing through plants; in some cases, the plants are almost too intimate, especially when covered with morning dew. Visitors either like it, or they don't. Oh well!

So it goes with other garden tactile experiences. My arms, scarred from rose thorns, ache from pulling weeds; my fingernails are often crusted black with crumbly compost. The top of my head is burnt a little tender from my forgetting to wear a hat on a sunny day.

Whenever I go out to check my rain gauge or fill the bird feeder, I have to step from the coolness or warmth of my house onto a wooden deck, then down the steps, up a flagstone walk, and across a small area mulched with bark. This experience is repeated in reverse order as I trudge back to the house. But not only do I see, smell, hear, and sometimes taste things on my walk, I *feel* every step of the way—every material from the firm flagstones to the soft mulch and the "give" of the boards on the deck—*through my feet*.

I am in touch with everything, through the simple act of checking a rain gauge.

That's what tactile means.

Right Plant, Right Place

While there is room in Slow Gardening for folks who go way out of their way to grow challenging plants, such as hybrid roses, heirloom vegetables, and even fruit trees that require deft pruning, choosing pest-resistant, well-adapted plants is a no-brainer for most good gardeners.

Whenever possible, select and grow plants that not only look great

To Label, or Not to Label

Few gardeners even think about it, other than what to do with all those little picture plant tags that come with flowers and veggies.

I admit it: I don't use them, at least not around plants. Not that I can remember the names of all my plants, or even where I planted all of them. (How many bulbs have I sliced, while digging a hole for something new?) But in my garden tidy labels just get in my way or become outdated or lost.

But wait . . . I do have labels, in one spot. Right in the middle of a front bed is a collection of several dozen different plant labels, of all shapes, sizes, colors, and materials, which I have collected. I have expensive metal plant tags made of aluminum and copper and creative labels made from plastic spoons, cut-off window blinds, seashells, pottery shards, flat "river" rocks, round disks cut from tree limbs, and even dried magnolia leaves, all written on with weatherproof pens. Lots of quality information, on a stick.

They are all arranged very professionally in rows in a small, neatly mulched bed alongside my front walk. But when visitors bend over to see what's planted there, they discover—*nothing*! There's nothing planted there; it's just a very horticultural-looking garden hoax.

I have some very good garden friends who label all their plants, and that's fine—but I ask them to ponder this: Has anyone ever seen a magazine photograph of a garden that had labels?

and have positive landscape functions but also are well adapted to your soils and pest pressures. Plants that feel right at home can grow for decades with little or no care.

Include as many garden-quality native plants as possible, because they not only are well adapted to local conditions but also provide shelter and food for native wildlife. Consider planting a mixed hedgerow of flowering and fruit-bearing native and adapted small trees and large shrubs to extend the nesting and feeding season for wildlife. Create a "verge" or edge of fruiting vines and wildflowers.

In the rest of the landscape, group trees, shrubs, and flowers for easier maintenance; groups and masses of plants are easier to maintain than individual plants—especially if the plants are connected in large mulched or ground-cover beds.

Have Something Blooming or Colorful All Year

Gardeners in mild-winter areas have the best opportunities to enjoy flowers year-round. But even folks in cold climates can extend their normal outdoor growing season with greenhouses, indoor plants, and even regular outdoor plants selected for their winter interest. Many shrubs and trees bloom in late winter or early spring and have spectacular forms, bark, berries, or fruit in midwinter.

It is interesting to note that, because they want business all year, fast-food restaurants and gas stations often have landscapes that look good in the winter; they use interesting shrubs with colorful winter foliage, winter bulbs, or hard features to create interest in even the worst weather—often without the need for pesticides or high maintenance.

Make a point to drive around the older parts of your town and visit country gardens and local or regional botanic gardens in all seasons—including the dead of winter—to see what is possible to include the following year in your own garden.

Enjoy Your Garden at Night

With the autumn ending of daylight saving time in the US (summer time in the UK) comes near-total darkness just when many of us are getting home from work. After the evening dishes are put away, and we are caught up with the news on TV, few of us even want to go back outside—yet that is often when the most pleasant weather can be had.

That's when evening-blooming plants bring out the best in our gardens, turning nighttime into showtime. Some of my favorite flowers that bloom late in the afternoon and continue mostly through the night are four o'clocks, moonflower, evening primrose, night-blooming cereus (a tropical cactus), datura, night-blooming jasmine, nicotiana, and some of the tropical water lilies.

In addition to their interesting flowers, most evening bloomers also emit strong fragrances to attract late-afternoon hummingbirds and night-flying pollinators such as the huge "hawk" moths, which in themselves can be a source of amazement.

Complement these flowers by creating a moon garden complete with light-colored paths lined with light-colored border plants (artemisia, variegated liriope, and dusty miller come to mind), small bowls of reflective water, garden furniture painted with light colors, and bright garden sculptures.

To make it safer to move about at night, install low-voltage night lighting. It is easy and inexpensive to install and uses a fraction of the energy of (but is just as bright as) more dangerous electric lights. Night lighting can be put together easily using components from garden stores (a low-voltage transformer with a timer, a length of special top-of-the-ground wire, and clip-on lights).

Solar-powered night lighting is acceptable, but it's nowhere near as bright as low-voltage lighting, and it does not charge very well during our long periods of low light in the winter.

Evening-blooming plants extend the hours of pleasure a garden can offer.

Make sure night lights illuminate plants and steps, but don't position them so they shine directly into the eyes of visitors, who may be temporarily blinded and not as familiar as you are with where steps start—or end. Be sure to adjust the timer on the transformer throughout the seasons, and when daylight saving time makes its twice-yearly switch.

Include an Outdoor Work Area

A toolshed is de rigueur for most gardeners. Slow Gardeners in particular are notorious for our love of tools that do things well. And we are not always in a hurry. Yet there's almost nothing more distracting than having to haul stuff back and forth from a faraway garage or storage building; instead, create a special place—either hidden from view, or out in the open where you can be proud of what you do—that has all the tools and accessories you need, organized and out of the weather.

Potting soil, stacks of old pots, tools, hoses, and all the rest can look pretty natural when piled up inside a rustic toolshed. It's also a practical place to site a compost bin near.

Make sure that any fuel or pesticides are stored carefully, away from sparks or electric equipment, and locked up when required for safety (especially with children around). It's also prudent to keep dangerous, sharp, or expensive items under lock and key, away from curious children and prying eyes.

The potting and toolshed is yet another place to garden.

Gardeners in cold climates can extend their growing season with a hobby greenhouse.

For extra interest, as mentioned in chapter 3, plant a green roof on top of the toolshed, using succulents and other low-water plants. For a funky look, strew broken pottery and old tools in with the plants.

Any flat or nearly flat area, including the roof of your garden shed, arbor, or doghouse can be fitted with a raised edge, covered with plastic or a pond liner, and planted in low-maintenance, drought-hardy plants.

Easy plants include hardy ground covers, cascading herbs, small native wildflowers, ornamental grasses, sedums and succulents, and hardy bulbs.

A small backyard greenhouse—like those found in seemingly every garden in Europe—can be an outstanding outlet for your gardening interests, especially in the winter and early spring, or in the summer in regions where the climate may not be reliably warm enough to plant some heat-loving vegetables and herbs outdoors.

Carefully Select and Display Sculpture

In his garden, every man may be his
own artist without apology or explanation.
　　—Louise Beebe Wilder

Art isn't about just showing off your taste. As Thomas Moore put it in *Care of the World's Soul*, "As the poets and painters of centuries have tried to tell us, art is not about the expression of talent or the making of pretty things. It is about the preservation and containment of soul. It is about arresting life and making it available for contemplation. Art captures the eternal in the everyday, and it is the eternal that feeds the soul."

On a simpler level, yard art can be used as a strong design feature in the garden. As Andrew Jackson Downing, a tastemaker of nineteenth-century garden design, wrote, "A few strongly marked objects, either picturesque or simply beautiful, will often confer their character upon a whole landscape."

All good gardens have some sort of artwork. If you're not careful, herbaceous material can all run together visually. But an embellishment can draw your eye into the composition, holding you in the garden experience. Using sculptures as focal points or to create specific styles is one thing; but you can also use garden art to express your individuality—if you dare.

We would do well to heed a comment once made by Neil Odenwald, a landscape architecture professor: "It has *nothing* to do with the quality of the piece; aged concrete can look five hundred years old, and you can

Homemade whimsies like this bottle tree can be as effective in some garden styles as classical statuary.

get a million dollars of embellishment from a single well-placed urn."

Yet whimsy has its place. English garden designer John Brookes said, "If there were ever a place to laugh, it is in a garden. To suddenly come across an amusing piece placed among vegetation or by the side of a pool is always a great bonus."

After seeing the hundreds of classical sculptures at Versailles and the fantastic centuries-old topiaries (living sculptures) of Levens Hall gardens in England—none of which is readily available to garden-variety gardeners—I personally prefer vernacular, or homemade, garden art: scarecrows, bottle trees (dead trees festooned with colorful glass bottles), rusty garden implements, and the like.

Trouble is, there is no limit to how far you can take this concept; there is a fine line between expressing joie de vivre and just displaying a lot of junk. Some people don't know how to stop and end up creating a "total yard show" by over-accessorizing with all sorts of little miniature windmills, gnomes, flamingos, and plastic flowers.

On the other hand, who am I to criticize? Especially after hearing the sentiments of Donald Featherstone, who patented the first plastic pink flamingo in 1957: "Before plastic, only the wealthy could afford poor taste."

Landscape architect Richard Griffin once told me that he didn't think art had a function. "Not like a sprinkler system or arbor," he put it. "But now I realize that it adds color, texture, contrasts. Like using a solid scarf or belt with a patterned dress. It's color, where there is none, in a shade garden. It's shiny, like a reflective glass globe. It's a totally different texture. That's the secret in design—contrasts. Not necessarily color, or texture."

The real question isn't whether a particular garden feature should be considered art or ornament. What matters are its *surroundings*. Garden art can help boost a well-designed garden, but it is still part of the landscape, and it should both inspire and reflect what the gardener wants out of the garden.

GARDEN FOLLIES

Construction oddities used as over-the-top garden accessories have been around for centuries. Usually the extravagant ornamental structures have little or no real purpose other than being part of the scenery.

They range from whimsical architectural details or entire buildings (seashell houses, walls for no reason, bridges to nowhere, recreated garden ruins, miniature Stonehenges) to "stumperies"–grottos made out of piled-up tree stumps.

Basically, if it makes you stop and wonder "Why?" then it is likely a folly.

The main thing all follies have in common is that, even if the creators think otherwise, there is no *real* purpose–they are entirely useless. It may hurt the builder's pride to hear this, but if other people think it's a folly, then it is a folly. It's entirely in the eye of the beholder.

My planted "green roof" entry arbor could be considered a folly by my neighbors, but not to me. Which makes it a folly indeed.

Grow Your Own Plants

Heirloom plants wouldn't be heirloom plants today if someone along the line had not started saving and sharing them with others. Many are easy to grow, to share, and to keep alive by rooting cuttings, saving and sowing seed, or dividing mature plants into smaller clumps.

Sharing locally popular plants helps create a strong sense of place, as anyone who has visited the vastly different gardens of Florida and England can attest. It also preserves diversity in an age when the vast majority of garden centers carry only a limited selection of currently popular plants.

Plus, sharing plants keeps us in touch with other gardeners, who in turn help civilize both us and our gardens.

Sharing plants is a common human trait, regardless of our background.

The main thing is, don't keep things all to yourself: propagate enough plants for your own use and for friends or neighbors. As garden writer and personality Roger Swain puts it, "If you aren't growing enough plants to share with others, there is something terribly wrong!"

Grow Your Own Vegetables, Fruits, and Culinary Herbs

Not everyone wants an old-fashioned vegetable garden with long, skinny rows. But anyone can put a few attractive vegetable plants in amongst the regular flowers—in small spaces, raised beds, or containers—without having to use a power tiller. Peppers, determinate (bush-type) tomatoes, lettuces, eggplants, kale, even okra are good-looking as ornamental plants, and they are good to eat. Container-grown veggies can be easy for folks with limited space, but a larger, raised-bed "kitchen" garden can be downright beautiful year-round. Again, without needing to turn over the soil with a power tiller.

Outstanding herbs that double as pretty plants include rosemary, oregano, chives, garlic chives, Mexican tarragon (also called Mexican mint marigold), mints, garlic, sage, and bay laurel; all are hardy perennials either in the open garden or when planted in pots to be brought indoors in the winter. Basil and hot peppers are fantastic summer annuals that come in many shapes, colors, and intensities; parsley is a very attractive biennial that is hardy enough to winter over outside in many climates.

Fruit plants can also double as regular "yard" plants. Depending on your climate, you may be able to easily grow figs, blueberries, pomegranate, native plums, apples, pears, Oriental or American persimmons, grapes (with annual pruning), pawpaw, tree quince, elderberry, mulberry, and potted citrus (kumquats, satsumas, and lemons are the easiest to grow in pots). There are others, of course, but many require special pruning and, depending on your climate, regular pesticide applications.

Be sure to preserve some of the harvest to share with others. If a food shortage ever comes, those who know how to grow and preserve food may be spared a little suffering! Learn to freeze vegetables and herbs; to make fruit jellies, preserves, cider, and wine; to dry herbs or make herb vinegars; and to store hard-shell squash, onions, potatoes, apples, and other storage-type food from the garden.

Many vegetables and herbs are easily grown in even recycled containers.

An espaliered fig and other fruit plants can be attractive parts of the garden design.

Sex in the Garden

Summertime brings out questions from gardeners, and one that is the most difficult to answer with a straight face is about sex in the garden.

When you couple most folks' penchant for neat, orderly surroundings with a dearth of bees, butterflies, and hummingbirds in many urban gardens, you have a recipe for plant sterility. Which leads to fewer vegetables and fruits, which leads to questions about sex.

This isn't as important for wind-pollinated plants like corn and self-pollinating veggies like beans and peas, though during one summer in the stillness of my little English greenhouse I had to go around daily thumping stems and support poles on tomatoes, peppers, and eggplants to loosen the pollen and cause it to shed.

But many plants need more help than that. Some have separate male and female plants, and without both genders growing nearby and in bloom at the same time, and without wind or insects spreading the pollen from plant to plant, they are unable to produce fruits. This is why a lot of hollies fail to have winter berries; only the female plants can even make berries, and then only if pollen from a nearby male makes it to the female flowers in the spring.

Some plants have both male and female flowers on the same plant. Corn has the male "tassels" at the top, which shed pollen onto the female "silks" protruding from young corn ears. And squashes and cucumbers have separate male and female flowers on the same plants; male flowers are on simple stems, with female flowers on the end of what looks like small squash, cuke, or melon fruitlets. If insects don't do the work of carrying pollen from male to female, the little fruits-to-be simply shrivel up and fall off.

When bees are missing for one reason or another, you can pluck off an open male squash flower, peel off its petals, and use it like a yellow brush to dab pollen inside the open female flowers. Within days you will be eating fully formed fresh squash.

By the way, pollen from one type of squash will not affect the flesh or eating quality of another type, but if you save the seeds you will get some sort of weird hybrid. Which explains a lot of gardeners' finding oddball gourdlike things growing out of their compost bins every summer.

To avoid all this, simply plant lots of different flowers in your garden, which can help attract insect pollinators, which in turn can help your veggies out with much-needed pollination.

Design Your Garden for People

This, like most other topics in this chapter, is covered in a little more detail in other chapters, but it bears repeating. To put it bluntly, if you don't have an all-season place to sit in the garden, you simply won't sit out in the garden. And you will be largely stuck indoors, missing out on transient things like birds, fireflies, cool breezes, interesting smells, and other outdoor delights.

Install firm, dry paving for patios and walks to ensure easy access. Provide for shade in the summer and protection from cold winds in the winter. Paying attention to simple, commonsense requirements like these is what makes the garden come together, helping you get out and enjoy nature, the plants, the changing seasons, and everything you have done.

Install a fire pit and waterfall to provide sound, motion, and interest to the garden, and for untold hours of relaxation and entertainment. Use them as occasional relief from television, and you will find people talking about stuff they would not even think about while indoors.

Running, falling, splashing water creates a soft "white noise" background that helps us tune out traffic and other city sounds, and also helps prevent mosquitoes, which need still water for breeding. To save energy, put the pump for a waterfall on a timer—there's no need to run it all night.

To get the most sound out of a water-fall, have it fall over the mouth of a small cave made by laying a flat rock or other flat surface over side supports. A cave, even a few inches deep and a few inches high, can create a "mega-phone" effect—like cupping your hands around your mouth to direct and amplify your voice. Aim it toward where you will sit, and the waterfall will be much louder.

Water is an essential human need and should be featured in every good garden.

A fire pit should be large enough to hold firewood and still have open space around it to prevent sparks and hot coals from popping out onto nearby plants or mulch. Surround it with rocks, bricks, or a metal ring to make it look more purposeful when not in use. Keep firewood nearby and dry, and make sure a water source (if nothing else, a bucket of water) is handy in case your fire gets too exuberant and tries to get out of control.

Use Quiet Hand Tools When Appropriate

A garden is a place to work, a place to dig into the earth and bring forth life. It is also a place to drop to your knees and nurture young life and watch it mature.
—Thomas DeBaggio

Raking leaves by hand, at least for a short time, can turn this necessary chore into a pleasurable experience.

For getting a lot of work done quickly, there's nothing wrong with a good leaf blower, string trimmer, garden tiller, lawn mower, edger, or leaf shredder. But most of them are noisy fuel hogs; even electric ones need power and are limited by the length of their cords.

But every now and then, it's important to get personal with your garden by using a shovel, spade, or digging fork. Prune by hand with loppers and shears instead of using an electric hedge trimmer. Use a sharp collinear hoe to slice weeds just below the soil surface instead of chopping them with a lot of wasted effort.

For that matter, use a flat-bladed file to keep all your tools sharp—it makes a huge difference, as anyone who has ever changed razors in the middle of a shave can attest.

If you have a fairly small lawn, try one of the modern, lightweight reel-type push mowers, which are quiet and provide excellent exercise. Try using a leaf rake for a small area—you will appreciate not only the satisfying sound it makes but also the feel of it in your hands.

Convenience aside, lose the leaf blower and the leaf shredder. A gas-powered leaf blower can emit as much pollution in a year as eighty cars. Not to mention all the dust, pollen, mold, and other allergens that are thrown up into the air—and up your nose. And the noise generated by a blower fan, pushing winds up to two hundred miles per hour, can deafen you; many communities have either restricted blowers to those with noise levels below seventy decibels or banned them outright.

A blower is not inexpensive, and fuel costs add up quickly. Yet a good rake, which can last for years, costs under twenty bucks. And think about this: walking a leaf blower around the yard expends about 140 calories an hour; using a leaf rake burns off about 325 calories.

The same goes for power leaf shredders. If you have a big yard, you can find or make space for a leaf pile. If you don't have room for a leaf pile, how can you justify the expense and storage space a noisy leaf shredder will take, to be used just two or three times a year? Think about it.

So, unless you really need one of these noisy, expensive leaf shredders for making lots of mulch, simply make a bigger pile of leaves. It, too, will compost and break down into humusy leaf mold. Break up sticks and twigs and pile them in neat circles around trees, then fill those with leaves for a natural effect that looks like you really care for the environment.

Get Personal with Your Weather

The meterologists at the Weather Channel have no idea—just guesses—as to how much it rained in your garden. A simple rain gauge—you are its only moving part—will give you an accurate reading instantly, and checking it gets you outside for a few minutes, during which time you can see for yourself what kind of weather your garden is experiencing.

Make a little sun tea. Put some teabags or fresh mint in a clear glass jug filled with clean, fresh water, and set it out on the porch to steep in the sun for a few hours. Clotheslines, once found in every single garden, have become almost passé; they are actually banned in some commu-

Raking Leaves
—Or Not

One of my neighbors is a young medical doctor, a busy bachelor in his first-ever home and garden that includes a huge oak, the kind with great big leaves that can fill over four dozen leaf bags. Last autumn, after he did a great job of raking, I pointed up into the tree and showed him that only about a third of the foliage had dropped. He looked crestfallen.

"How long will I have to do this?" he asked. I said, "The rest of your life."

In the woods, leaves naturally compost and recycle their nutrients back into the trees and woodland wildflowers. But on the lawn they just mat down and smother the grass over the winter.

Some folks theorize that a layer of leaves will insulate and protect the lawn from harsh winter weather. But, in fact, it's just the opposite; at best the loose blanket will keep the grass tender past the first few frosts, but too tender to survive a real deep freeze.

In other words, you can't use that as an excuse not to rake.

Another reason giving for not raking is that composted leaves recycle nutrients. There is a lot to that, but only in the long haul, after the leaves have been broken down by weather or foot traffic and begun to compost or get eaten and pulled into the soil by worms. But that happens best in warmer weather, so there is a several-month period when they just lie there.

If you do decide not to rake, the best alternative strategy is to run the mower over the leaves, breaking them into smaller bits that will filter more quickly down to the soil line, where they will compost more quickly or make bite-sized meals for worms. Plus, mowing makes it at least look like you are doing something good.

nities as being "tacky." (What would your grandmother have said about *that*?) Yet there are few things in life more satisfying than putting on jeans and a T-shirt that have dried in the sun and the fresh air; the little bit of scratchiness will put you in touch with your body, and might make you feel a little better about yourself.

Some neighbors will think it's tacky, but you can hold your head high knowing that no electricity—generated from some artificial energy source—was used to dry your jeans, sheets, tennis shoes, socks, and other clothes.

Clotheslines save incredible amounts of energy (and the related costs) and wear and tear on both clothes dryers and the clothes themselves (where do you think all that stuff in the lint trap comes from?), and using them makes

No carbon was used in the drying of these jeans.

your clothes smell better. You will feel better, too.

Note: There are numerous advocates working together on a state-by-state level to have legislation passed that bans restrictions and covenants against "energy conservation devices"—including clotheslines and solar collectors.

Also, plant vines on an arbor over the patio or deck and on west-facing walls to help keep the sun from overheating the house during hot weather. Deciduous vines lose their leaves in the fall; they let the warm winter sun in but provide cool shade during the heat of summer. And they completely block solar heat gain on otherwise exposed walls and paving. Fast-growing annual vines such as gourds, hyacinth bean, and moonflower can give quick relief while long-lived climbing hydrangea, roses, grapes, and wisteria take several years to really fill in.

Lastly, install a small solar energy system. This can be used to charge batteries that power the garden's night lighting and even the water garden pump. Maybe there will be enough left over to run a small fan—

or even your laptop computer. The kinds of systems used on small boats work just fine in gardens as well.

Garden to Encourage Year-Round Wildlife

Having butterflies, hummingbirds, songbirds, and singing frogs is a nice side benefit to having a full garden. If you have enough shrubs and trees to provide cover for wildlife, they will use it, and usually nest in it as well. But you can add to this by putting up birdhouses, or half-burying a clay pot on its side as a toad house, or making a brush pile for small ground-dwelling animals, insects, and other critters.

You can even consider putting up a bat house—creepy, perhaps, but more effective against night-flying insects than a noisy, stinky bug zapper! A single bat will eat more mosquitoes in one night than an entire colony of purple martin birds—really. But migrating purple martins, like bluebirds and other species whose natural habitats have been severely depleted, depend on us for housing, be it in the form of a hollowed-out gourd or a wooden house placed on a fence post.

Plans and instructions for these birdhouses are usually available online from wildlife resources, including the National Wildlife Federation, which also certifies gardens as official "Backyard Wildlife Habitats," complete with a neat little sign to put up so your neighbors think you are having all this stuff for a reason. Which you are, of course, but it helps to have an official seal of approval in plain view of naysayers.

Other than natural shelter or man-made housing, all it takes to have a complete wildlife habitat is food and water.

Include a well-stocked bird feeder. This is a simple way to attract motion, color, and even drama to your garden. Bird feeders can be used all year, even when wild birds have plenty of food in the brush.

A bird feeder can be any kind or style, though many gardeners have learned to appreciate so-called squirrel-proof feeders (good luck with them; squirrels are a lot craftier than you'd expect). I prefer a simple, open, platform-type feeder with raised sides to keep bird seed from blowing off when big birds land on the feeders.

Plant it and they will come. Add plants that attract butterflies, bees,

Phenology

When I noticed a neighbor's Japanese magnolia fully budded with some flowers already opening up, I knew what it meant: *it's going to freeze, soon*. Happens nearly every spring, almost as if the flowers' opening *causes* a freeze.

Without taking into account climate change or habitat destruction, these kinds of natural events generally occur around the same times every year, leading farmers and gardeners to depend on them as informal dates on subtle natural calendars. The practice of watching for natural signals—studying recurring plant and animal life-cycle events, such as when certain plants flower, caterpillars emerge from hibernation, or birds begin to migrate or build nests—is called *phenology*.

Bird lovers watch eagerly for the first hummingbirds before putting up feeders, and for early purple martin "scouts" to arrive before cleaning out and putting up gourd houses.

While northern and midwestern gardeners have to wait until Memorial Day to start planting summer flowers and vegetables, southerners traditionally start to plant on Good Friday, because that's when the last frost of the season is usually past and the soil is warm enough to keep seeds from rotting in the cold and damp ground. You can also watch for fishermen to start sitting on the bare riverbanks instead of on their bait buckets—that's a sure sign the soil has warmed up.

Because of allergies, I begin stocking up on antihistamines when I first start seeing pine pollen on my truck's windshield. And I know that when the azaleas start to bloom, I can start walking barefoot outdoors, toughening up my winter-tender soles before summer. But as soon as roses begin to bloom, I put on my flip-flops to keep from getting bee stings in my feet as I walk through the clover.

That is one kind of phenology that is worth paying attention to.

and hummingbirds, all of which are very important for pollination, as well as for our entertainment. These creatures are a sign of a healthy garden, and they *need* sources of pollen and nectar for food, especially in highly developed urban areas. Plus, they often eat caterpillars and other insects that damage the garden (even hummingbirds eat tiny insects for the protein they can't get from flower nectar).

Try to include flowering and berry-laden plants as close to all year long as possible. After all, wildlife can't just sit around waiting for you to fill the feeder when you may be cooped up indoors or on vacation! Even winter weeds in the lawn—notably dandelion, henbit, wild onion and garlic, and chickweed—provide nectar and pollen for the bees and little butterflies that emerge during sunny, warm spells in midwinter through early spring. Without your lawn weeds, those little creatures might starve!

While we're on the subject of bees, consider this: urban beekeeping can be a most interesting and beneficial hobby, without your having to become a full-fledged beekeeper. Simple home hives are easy to set up, and it is fairly easy to harvest your own "homegrown" honey (which can be swapped or bartered with neighbors for other garden plants and produce).

Just don't put a beehive—or the kinds of plants that attract bees—near a path or doorway; you don't want guests or the mail carrier to feel creeped out by having to avoid flying stingers.

The main point here is that, even without our going the unnatural (but interesting) route of deliberately feeding wildlife, natural food sources are easy enough to provide. A wide variety of shrubs, trees, and other plants—especially natives, which are most attractive to native wildlife—have flowers with nectar, berries, and other fruit. And there will be enough little bugs on your flowers to keep beneficial critters busy and full.

Water is also crucial for wildlife, whether they get it in your garden or have to take a break and find it elsewhere. *This is important year-round—including in the winter when normal sources of water may be frozen.*

To help birds, butterflies, and bees, all you need is a simple birdbath, or a shallow pool made from an upside-down trashcan lid partly sunk in the ground. Dripping water—which attracts birds from a surprising distance—can be as simple as a plastic water jug suspended above the bird bath with the tiniest hole you can make with the tip of a pin; it will drip slowly for many hours. In cold winter climates, you can keep the water in a bird bath unfrozen by placing a small electric immersion heater in it; these don't use a lot of energy, and they fit well into the kind of small-scale solar electric system that you use for night lighting and other garden uses.

Don't worry about mosquitoes breeding in a deliberately placed water feature: you have them already in your garden, so it's not a huge deal. Besides, birds will actually eat some of the larvae.

Butterflies, which cannot land right on water, are attracted to the edges of water features but can be helped by adding a handful of gravel to one side where they can land. And they will also gather in surprising numbers on saucers of moist sand or even mud, on which they "puddle" for the moisture they sip with their tonguelike proboscis.

Toads and frogs must have water for mating and laying eggs, and for their tadpoles to survive for a few weeks. If you have a water garden, expect to have lots of these nocturnal, bug- and slug-eating natives (*warning:* they can be very loud singers during mating season). You can even create a temporary pool by laying plastic sheeting in a low area and keeping it filled with water from a hose until the tadpoles mature.

Lastly, learn to make peace with critters you don't like. The cute critters, including butterflies, dragonflies, hummingbirds, and other

birds, are to be expected, even greedy, flea-bitten squirrels are interesting to watch. But others, though serving useful roles in their niches, are difficult to accept; wasps, snakes, and mice come to mind. I don't especially like them, but they do have their purposes, and I tolerate them—as long as they mind their business and stay out of household mischief.

Anyone who thinks he doesn't have these animals, and more, in his garden is fooling himself. Out of sight, out of mind doesn't mean *nonexistent*. Luckily, most of the critters in the garden are extremely beneficial, even if we don't particularly want to pick them up.

If you don't like surprises, try gardening with a little stick in hand, and use it to rattle and rustle shrubs and ground covers as you move about; this can help ward off unexpected encounters with wasps, spiders, little garden snakes, and other lurking wildlife.

As for mammal control—for deer, raccoons, rabbits, moles, voles, squirrels, rats, mice, groundhogs, pocket gophers, skunks, bears, armadillos, possums, coyotes, neighborhood cats, and all the others that you probably don't appreciate when they tear up your garden—believe me on this: regardless of what anyone may try to sell you, the bottom line is fencing. If there were other dependable ways to control them, we would all know about it by now.

Repellents may work for some folks, for a while, but fencing (and/or humane trapping and removal) is about the only strategy we can depend on. Sorry.

Attracting and enjoying wildlife in the garden—birds, butterflies, bees, toads and frogs, little snakes, lizards, squirrels, and more—is easier than most people realize. Your attitude toward some or all of the wildlife and their activities can make or break your enjoyment of the garden itself.

A well-rounded garden can attract a wide variety of wildlife.

Make Compost

Composting, which is covered in more detail in chapter 5, can be a very interesting long-term hobby that improves the quality of both your garden soil and your experience and attitude toward your garden.

It doesn't have to look fancy, unless you want it to. It can simply be a neat leaf pile, left alone to work on its own schedule. Or you can install a simple bin, filled with leaves, shredded cardboard, kitchen scraps, and other degradable ingredients.

There's no need to be a fast composter, either—*it ain't a race*! As mentioned in chapter 5, my friend Joe Keyser summed it up neatly: "There are only two rules for good composting: Stop throwing all that stuff away, and pile it up somewhere." The rest is pure finesse.

Keep it organized and neat. It's one thing to put a compost bin near the kitchen door, but quite another to make it look neat and not smell bad or attract unwanted night visitors.

Braver souls can also try vermicomposting (composting with worms)—as interesting and entertaining an indoor activity as caring for any potted plant. To harvest some of the finest compost on earth (worm castings), shred up some newspapers, and mix them with chopped vegetable and fruit kitchen scraps, plus eggshells and coffee grounds, and put them in a large sweater-box-sized container full of "red wiggler" worms.

Don't worry about odors—if the worms are happy and working away, the whole operation will only smell like wet paper.

Reuse or Recycle Materials Everywhere You Can

Whether you reuse pots, make a bench out of an old wooden door, or make a walkway out of broken concrete, there are TONS of opportunities to recycle stuff in the garden.

In fact there are too many to mention right here, but a quick list could include making planters from tires; lining your flower beds with bottles stuck neck-down; building a sturdy retaining wall from stacked tires painted to look like dirt, filled with soil, and planted with an evergreen shrub like heavenly bamboo (*Nandina domestica*); making a birdhouse

Recycled is recycled—a used tire is as valid a planter as a half whiskey barrel.

out of old fence planks and a license plate for its roof; creating a wall sculpture from rusted garden tools; or planting flowers in a broken wheelbarrow.

To fellow "dumpster divers" the list is endless.

Visit Public Botanic Gardens

Whenever you're on vacation, try to take advantage of the interesting displays of plants set out by earnest horticulturists and plant lovers, in botanic gardens and public parks. These "botanical zoos" often have astounding collections of unique plants, but they usually also have small vignettes of locally hardy beauties that, because of staff and budget cuts, are often barely maintained—offering insights into great plant combinations of low-input plants.

You can meet like-minded people at these botanic gardens and usually will be able to attend educational sessions as well.

While you're at it, walk around older neighborhoods, particularly the established ones where gardeners are active and don't "outsource" their chores to professionals. This is where you will find the most interesting mix of plants and garden styles, and methods for dealing with problems in mature landscapes where the original foundation plantings (the tightly pruned gumdrop- and meatball-shaped shrubs put up close to the house when it was first built) have long since petered out.

You will see more variety with more seasonal color, and less senseless maintenance of plants and garden styles that simply no longer fit modern lifestyles.

Take a minute to chat up people you find out gardening. Rarely are gardeners unwilling to explain what they are doing and why; often, in

COLLECT AND USE RAINWATER

A rain barrel is as easy as can be. Make one out of a large trashcan fitted with a faucet and rubber gaskets. Cut a hole in the top to put your downspout into, and cover the hole with hardware cloth to keep out leaves and mosquitoes.

Create a "rain garden" sump. Where there is a low area in your landscape, make it more deliberate and create a way for rainwater to get to it, where it can slowly percolate into the ground instead of running off into the storm sewer. Around the area, plant Louisiana iris, ornamental grasses, cannas, and other "bog" plants that tolerate occasional wet feet.

Even a small homemade rain barrel connects the gardener with larger environmental issues.

fact, they are willing—even pleased—to share some plants with you as well.

And remember, you can't get or give a plant from someone else's hand without touching their hand or mind.

Support Your Local Farmers' Market

Patronizing your local farmers' market is the easiest way to make sure you get the freshest vegetables, fruits, herbs, and other garden products in season and from local growers. Sure, they often supplement what they offer for sale with items from other growers, often from other states, but

Farmers' markets put consumers in direct contact with local growers.

they do so reluctantly, and try to make what they offer as fresh and local as possible.

While visiting Terra Madre, the biennial Slow Food event in Turin, Italy, I spent a lot of time browsing through hundreds of vendors at the nearby Salone del Gusto, the world's largest small-scale market. Small artisanal food producers from all over the world were displaying and selling breads, vegetables, herbs, spices, meats, fish, cheeses, wines, olive oils, garden tools, and more—all made or produced sustainably, often using ancient practices that help to keep both local food specialties and traditions alive.

Taking a "locavore" approach in our purchasing habits not only saves on transportation and storage expenses but also helps encourage more local growers to produce even more of our food locally, throughout the growing season and, increasingly, throughout the year. This, in turn, keeps money circulating more "slowly" to other businesses and individuals within the community in a positive feedback loop.

Take Advantage of Area Garden Education

It's one thing to take advantage of the tremendous resources in garden books, magazines, and online garden sites, but there are also huge opportunities to be found locally. You can easily tap into the resources of state university horticulturists, their master gardener volunteers, garden clubs, plant societies, local colleges, garden centers, and botanical gardens; all offer gardening seminars, how-to demonstrations, night classes, lectures (often by high-end national experts), flower shows, garden tours, plant sales and swaps, and sometimes even personal design or diagnostic visits to private gardens.

In addition, local garden experts usually write for newspapers and host call-in question-and-answer radio programs; many also have regular newsletters or online blogs. Most of the better online garden sites have regional contributors who address local gardening issues and answer questions with very region-specific answers.

Take full advantage of these many local resources not only to keep abreast of what is happening in your area but also to find out about more opportunities to meet and learn from these experienced local garden experts.

Keep a Garden Journal or Blog

My horticulturist great-grandmother used to write almost daily in her journals of what was blooming, which birds were appearing, when she did certain chores, and what she was thinking about, garden-wise. Reading these journals nearly a century after they were written, I discover that a lot of the same events are happening in my own garden—which is a real comfort, learning that I am not really plowing new ground, but instead am following in the footsteps of gardeners who dug in the ground before me.

I can also review things I wrote in my own journals during the same months over several years and get a good idea of what I can expect during the same month next year.

Keeping a journal—or an online blog—about daily observations and thoughts can help settle a gardener down and see things both in the here-and-now and over the long run.

Photographs of your garden taken one year can give you a

Gardening is an original wireless contact with the real world.

Sun Dogs and Rainbows

Not long ago I got my second-ever sighting of a "sun dog"—a rainbow-colored spot just to one side of the sun. And no, I wasn't having a heat-stroke—in fact, I pointed it out to several friends and photographed it for proof.

I've always been fascinated by rainbows, but sun dogs are unique and somewhat rare, caused by flat ice crystals in the sky that act as prisms and create a somewhat roundish or oblong spot of color at the same altitude as the sun. My sun dog was reddish on the sun side, but the spot went quickly through orange into blue before trailing out as white.

A rainbow is simply light refracted through water drops. To see this effect indoors, set a glass of water so it barely hangs over the edge of a window, and hold a white sheet of paper below it to see the rainbowlike spectrum. Maybe have kids color its different bands.

Actually, though human eyes tend to see distinct color bands, a rainbow gradually spans a continuous spectrum of colors. And, except with double rainbows, where the color scheme is mirrored and inverted, they are always in the same order: red, orange, yellow, green, blue, indigo, and violet (most schoolkids learned this with the mnemonic name of Roy G. Biv).

Making a small rainbow outdoors is easy. Just hold a hose so you (and the kids) have your back to the sun and the spray is below eye level with a dark background (trees, hedges, even the lawn). Using a fine nozzle—or just a thumb, to keep things simple—spray downward; the rainbow will appear just above the spray. *Hints:* move the hose around a bit to find the best effect, and make the spray as fine as possible for a clearer, larger rainbow.

When the kids get into school and start learning about prisms and colors, they will remember who first taught them how to make their own.

hugely valuable perspective just a year or two later, and help you appreciate what has actually been done in the interim. And it can remind you of plants from the past, long gone for one reason or another.

Keeping a record of what you do and think in the garden helps ground you in what you are doing both now and in the future.

Share with Children

Can you remember the first person who ever showed you something in a garden, and could actually explain it to you in words you could understand?

Digital used to mean using your fingers for stuff besides texting. It's time to help out some kids—and maybe some Blackberry-addicted adults—with some real-life lessons from hands-on gardening.

This is one of the most important tenets of Slow Food: putting young people into gardens so they can experience real life, and teaching them where food comes from, and how to grow it themselves.

My horticulturist great-grandmother, a charter member of her garden club in the 1930s, taught me even into my teens to notice and discern small, subtle things, like the differences between caterpillars. She encouraged me to make value judgments, such as how a plant in one part of her garden could be considered a cherished wildflower, while the same plant in another area was a weed.

She showed me how to tell a jonquil from other daffodils and used row upon row of flowers to instill organizational skills and orderliness (this lesson, unfortunately, didn't "take").

One of my grandmothers was a blue-ribbon garden club lady who taught me diligence and elegance. My other grandmother was a simple hill-country gardener who loved her zinnias and proudly accessorized her flowers with a painted concrete chicken (which I have in my garden today). From her I learned to take pride in simple things.

My mother made me drag potted plants indoors and out every time the weather changed, but she also introduced me to birds, and worms, and how to catch fish and little turtles in the bayou.

Other older gardeners taught me about generosity through plant sharing. My grandfather showed me how to step on pecans to see if they were firm enough to pick up or if they broke because they were "faulty" and rotten inside, and my father taught me to get chores done before going out to play. Raking leaves and mowing grass (which of course I *hated*) provided a sense of accomplishment, however grudging.

Get it? These folks, by making me do simple chores around the garden, taught me some important life skills in little ways that affect my outlook to this day.

There are endless opportunities to help children and new gardeners interact with the world through gardening, without getting so technical it bores them or burns them out.

As an easy example, do you remember that child's game using a piece of string tied in a loop, and turned and twisted into various shapes such as "cup and saucer"? Those games have survived being shown from child to child to child over many years and across many cultures, *without ever having been written down* in a how-to book, spreading like a precursor to Internet viruses. *Gardening gone viral!*

It doesn't take a lot of planning to change a child's life with gardening. A few easy interactions include:

- Having children (your own or even those of neighbors) breathe in the heady fragrances of different flowers, then getting them to tell you what they smell like.
- Having them look at flower petals, leaves, or maybe an insect through a magnifying glass.
- Showing a child how to make a rainbow in thin air, using the fine mist of water made with a thumb over the end of a garden hose.
- Helping a young gardener plant something that has instant gratification, such as mint for making mint tea, or bulbs that are all but guaranteed to grow and bloom.
- Getting their creative juices going by painting a flower on a seashell or rock.
- Helping them make a scarecrow and then having everyone tell a made-up story about it.
- Getting a young gardener to help pick some fresh herbs, cut them up, and put them into a spaghetti or chili sauce, to see where flavors come from.

• Taking a child—or a young adult—to a farmers' market to see the incredible variety of vegetables, fruits, herbs, and other garden products that are locally grown or made, and to meet the people who actually brought them from the farm.

Schoolchildren in Ghana take classes in growing locally adapted vegetables.

• Showing someone why snapdragons are called that (if you don't know, it's because a grownup never took time to show *you*!).

• If nothing else, simply bending over with a child and wiggling your fingers in the grass or mulch, and talking about whatever you discover. Ask more questions than you answer.

This is all it takes to put a child in touch with the *real world*—as opposed to staring at and punching buttons on a handheld electronic keyboard.

Do you know some children in the neighborhood who need this informal sort of instruction? By spending a little time pointing out small details, you can change a child's outlook toward the outdoors (and maybe even get a little help with chores).

When school is out for summer vacation, most kids won't be out playing in the yards like they did when I was a kid. There are too many "cooler" things to do now, indoors and out. So it's even more crucial to snag those children we can, when we can, and teach them life skills from the garden.

School Gardens, Outdoor Classrooms

With an emphasis on teaching children comes a desire to set up school gardens. However, most school districts do not include gardening in the curriculum, so only a few such gardens with motivated teachers or parents actually succeed.

There are two major approaches to youth gardening, both with strong advocates, and everyone agrees that the two should find common ground: food production/education and environmental studies. Fortunately, both approaches can be used in the same outdoor teaching space.

Curriculum needs aside, there are a few *design features* found in most successful school/youth gardens around the country. The American Horticulture Society has organized the National Youth Gardening program, which has annual conferences, workshops, and Web-based advice.

While working with a team of nationally recognized youth garden experts to design a functional demonstration children's garden at Disney's Epcot Center in Orlando, Florida, I gleaned the following "big ideas" that are found in every successful youth garden, regard-less of size or funding:

Hands-on gardening activities inspire curiosity about nature, even in very young children.

- Enclosure, including walls and a kid-sized, kid-designed entry, which gives the garden a sense of being a "special place" and also provides a sense of security.
- Access to water (with a hard surface to keep feet dry) and electricity (with a ground-fault circuit interrupter for safety).
- Firm walkways (for wet weather and for access by the disabled).
- Teaching area (classroom setting, partially walled off from the rest of the garden) with shaded seating that stays dry.
- A roomy potting bench, and tool and equipment storage (can double as seating).
- Signs, charts, maps, and other teaching tools; an outdoor erasable chalkboard.
- Raised beds and various large containers for planting.

- A weather station to record rainfall, temperature, wind, time (human sundial), etc.
- A water garden (usually small, with easy access for experiments).
- Vertical structures (for vines, banners, art, and a greater sense of enclosure).
- Smaller enclosed areas for special lessons (composting, plant starting, worm box, private student counseling, visitors' viewing area).
- Varying elevations (may incorporate a tunnel, slide, bridge, etc.).
- Lots of color, texture, sound, and other sensory considerations.
- A wildlife area with bird feeders, bird houses, butterfly plants (non-bee!), etc.
- Art (multimedia; can be incorporated in all the other design features).
- Widely varying plants to fit curriculum needs (beyond mere food production).

A few examples of types of plants to include are those that are historic, fast-growing, fragrant, wildlife attracting (bird and butterfly), tasty (herbs and vegetables), geographically or culturally linked (Native American, African, South American, Asian, etc.), shade producing, and of economic value (cotton, pine, etc.)

Note: All plants *must* perform during the school year or be able to survive the summer without supplemental care. Also, food plants should be emphasized.

There are many other considerations, of course, but these are commonly found in nearly every successful outdoor classroom with garden components.

Note: While youth should be involved in as many aspects of design as possible, *every* consideration must be given to *safety* (to avoid sharp edges, falls, bee stings, poisonous plants and seeds, etc.) and *maintenance.* This *cannot* be overstated!

Ponder the Mysteries of the Universe

The closer you look at something, the more you see. The microcosm that exists in your own backyard has infinite mysteries and miracles, successes and tragedies. It's a bug-eat-bug world filled with living, breathing creatures as bizarre as anything a science fiction writer could ever dream up.

It's a place where some things thrive and others fade away, where there are constant struggles between thugs and victims, including both plants and animals. A garden can force us to learn valuable lessons about firm lines drawn in the dirt and the inevitable compromises that have to be made. And we are given insights into our own character—and that of family and friends. It's where we learn our place in the Big Picture.

It doesn't take much to start noticing how beautifully compli-cated even the simplest garden can be.

The garden is where the world comes together in myriad intricate ways.

Do Better

Maybe you can't change the whole world. But by slightly modifying the way you garden, you can change your own yard, and your own mind and attitude. And that's a start.
  —Steve Bender

As the ancient Stoic philosophers knew, the sun is going to rise and set no matter what we do, but we can choose to some extent what we do in our daily habits.

By making minor adjustments in how we approach our gardens—including but not limited to the items just covered in this chapter—we can make little changes here and there that barely affect our daily lives but have a major impact on the bigger picture.

Especially when we gently share our enthusiasm with others. Especially children.

In the end, it is you, the gardener, who decides what you should do, and how, and even if what you want is worth the effort at all.

Remember, the Slow Gardening approach is *gestalten*, meaning that you are the central figure in your garden. The more you know what you want to do, the more focused you can be on the here and now and take responsibility for what happens.

To paraphrase iconic 1960s rock guitarist Jimi Hendrix, "You're the one who's gotta go when it's your time to go, so feel free to *garden the way you want to.*"

Everything is important. —Dr. Who

INDEX

ABOUT THE AUTHOR

Felder Rushing is a tenth-generation hands-in-the-dirt American gardener. He has been a national director of the Garden Writers Association, member of the National Youth Gardening Committee, past president of several horticulture societies, and distinctly non-stuffy board member of the American Horticultural Society. He is a longtime garden columnist, popular lecturer nationwide and overseas, host of a National Public Radio–affiliate program, and the author or coauthor of sixteen books including the award-winning *Passalong Plants.*

ABOUT THE FOREWORD AUTHOR

Roger B. Swain is the host emeritus of PBS's *The Victory Garden* and author of *The Practical Gardener.*

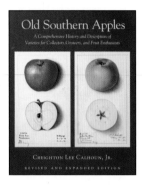
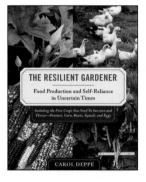
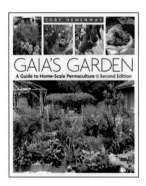
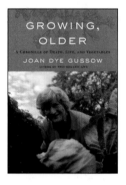